Early Praise for *Debugging TypeScript Applications*

An approachable, practical guide to debugging TypeScript applications—perfect for developers looking to build real debugging experience.

➤ **Berci Varga**
Product engineer, Framer

A calm, battle-tested guide to debugging modern TypeScript apps. Andrey Ozornin shows you how to make failures loud and fixes fast in the best possible way.

➤ **Constant Druon**
Product engineer, Framer

Debugging TypeScript Applications

Build Web Apps That Don't Break

Andrey Ozornin

The Pragmatic Bookshelf
Dallas, Texas

See our complete catalog of hands-on, practical, and Pragmatic content for software developers:
https://pragprog.com

Sales, volume licensing, and support:
support@pragprog.com

Derivative works, AI training and testing, international translations, and other rights:
rights@pragprog.com

ISBN-13: 9798888651988
Book version: P1.0—May 2026

Contents

Acknowledgments

I don't believe in "self-made men." Look closer at any success story, and you will find a whole crowd of very different people. Much like in a Breugel's painting, the closer you look, the more people you notice. They teach, inspire, protect, push, advise, believe in you, correct you, and simply show up at the right moment. It takes a village to raise a child, and I'm lucky to have found myself in a cozy one, full of kind, supportive people who made publishing this book possible.

I want to thank my development editor, Kelly Talbot, for guiding me through the whole writing process that took over a year and for correcting my English grammar, which is sometimes just embarrassing. Thanks to the executive editor, Susannah Davidson, and the acquisition editor, Margaret Eldridge, for seeing potential in this book and signing me for my first book. Special kind words go to The Pragmatic Programmers founder Dave Thomas. Being able to work side by side with these people feels like being invited into a royal court, no less.

My amazing coworkers at Framer[1] did an excellent technical review of the book. A grand merci à Constant Druon, a bow to performance ninja Ivan Akulov, praise to web artist Berci Varga, and special thanks to my teammate and a data structure hero Ryan Dainton. They caught some sneaky mistakes, pointed out missing bits, and helped give the book that final polish. Okay, I admit these people might have had a bit of an ulterior motive—if I get better at debugging, they'll have fewer problems.

My wife, Daria Chetvernya, supported every step of my way: she gave me more room when I needed it, a gentle nudge when I was stuck, and a helping hand when I felt down.

1. https://www.framer.com

If you'll allow me the luxury of giving you life advice, I would like to say one thing: find the people empowering you, and do your best to empower them. It's the most rewarding thing you can do as a professional and as a human.

Welcome

If there's software, there are bugs. No exceptions. You open a small static text-only website in a browser with a sophisticated rendering engine running on an incredibly complex operating system, on hardware working on the edge of what's possible within the limitations of physics as we know it today, and each of these layers of complexity contains errors. Maybe, except the physics.

More code means more bugs, and writing new code is the easiest part of software engineering. Even before the rise of AI coding agents and copilots, our industry had been overly focused on writing new code. We wrote dozens of legendary books on design patterns, created powerful tools simplifying writing and reading code, asked candidates to code from scratch on every other job interview, and published thousands of comprehensive step-by-step tutorials about building all sorts of applications from scratch.

Building products is the most important outcome of software engineering, but it's not the most valuable skill for a software engineer. What is more valuable? Understanding how a complex system works. Picking the most impactful and meaningful development work. Saving the day when a critical incident arises at 3 a.m. Building systems that won't break at 3 a.m., that are easy to maintain, and that are safe to work with. We'll be covering it all in this book.

Strong debugging skills are good for your mental health. When you resolve an issue, you feel fulfilled, and it gives you control and confidence. When you don't, you feel helpless. The better you resolve problems, the better you sleep.

Is This Book for Me?

This book is for front-end or full-stack engineers who ship JavaScript/TypeScript to browsers. If you're a junior or middle developer looking to advance your career or ensure job security, this book is a right fit. No PhD in computer science is required—just curiosity, an IDE like VS Code or WebStorm, and a willingness to read a couple more console logs. This book is a practical, down-to-earth guide you can complete in a week to help you become a better developer delivering better software.

What's in This Book?

In Chapter 1, Printing and Interpreting Errors, on page 1, you'll learn to recognize common error types and use code overrides in Chrome Developer Tools. In Chapter 2, Setting Guardrails with Throw and Catch, on page 15, you'll learn to intentionally use exceptions to build fail-fast and fault-tolerant systems. Chapter 3, Prioritizing Bugs, on page 29, will teach you to estimate bugs and choose the most impactful work by using RICE methodology. Next, we'll explore root cause analysis techniques and ways of finding a stable bug reproduction in Chapter 4, Finding the Root Cause, on page 39. After that, we'll discover modern tools that can help you to build reliable, maintainable software in Chapter 5, Designing Software That Doesn't Break, on page 53. In Chapter 6, Following the Data Flow, on page 77, we'll get hands-on again and will take a close look at interactive debugging in Chrome developer tools. You'll be surprised what it's capable of. Chapter 7, Debugging Asynchronous Operations, on page 99, will explore debugging network interactions, workers, and other asynchronous operations like timers. Finally, in Chapter 8, Make Your Code Debuggable, on page 113, we'll discuss error monitoring, alerting, structured logging, and leaving performance traces that will make your code transparent and save you tons of time when debugging any new issue.

How to Read This Book

How should you read this book? Relaxed and with pleasure. You'll get the most out of this book if you follow along with the exercises. You'll need a computer for all chapters except Chapter 3, Prioritizing Bugs, on page 29, and Chapter 4, Finding the Root Cause, on page 39. In some chapters, I use small, silly games I built specially for this book. They're available on GitHub, and it's better if you clone them and follow along using them. I made those games not because they're particularly typical examples but because they were fun to code and they serve the purpose of illustrating the concepts pretty well. You'll have to excuse me for that. Other than that, you're an adult and I respect your right to read this book however you want.

Before We Begin

> In a laboratory situation, when your whole procedure goes haywire, when everything goes wrong or is indeterminate or is so screwed up by unexpected results you can't make head or tail out of anything, you start looking laterally. ... Lateral knowledge is knowledge that's from a wholly unexpected direction, from a direction

The First Actual Case of a Bug Being Found

The team working on the Harvard Mark II computer in 1947 found a curious malfunction. They traced it to a particular relay and found a moth trapped inside it. They taped it in their logbook and labeled it as the "first actual case of bug being found."

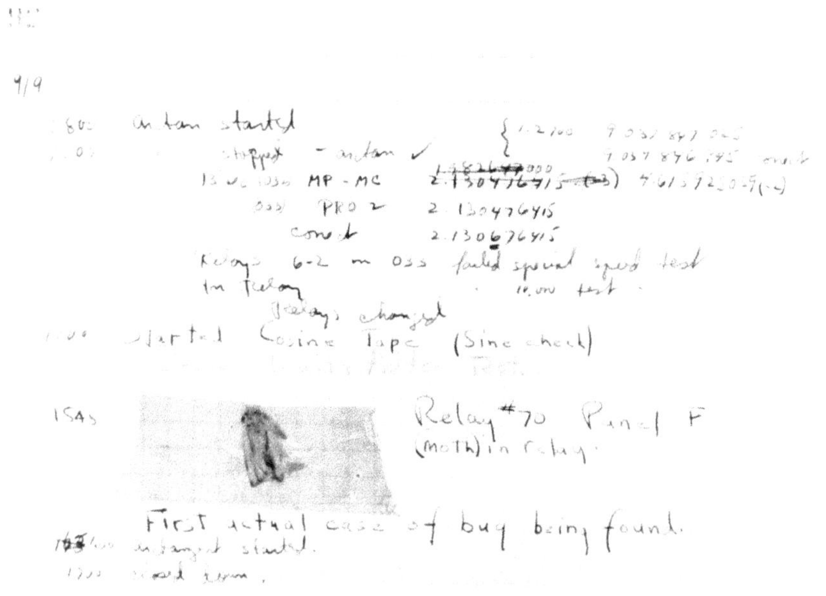

Contrary to popular belief, this story wasn't the first use of the word *bug* meaning technical malfunction. Engineers had been finding and fixing bugs for over a hundred years by then. Thomas Edison, telephone pioneers, and journalists during WWII used the word "bug" to describe such problems. The Mark II operators knew the term and made some wordplay around the bug caused by a real insect. Still, nice one.

> that's not even understood as a direction until the knowledge forces itself upon one. Lateral truths point to the falseness of axioms and postulates underlying one's existing system of getting at truth. *—Zen and the Art of Motorcycle Maintenance: An Inquiry into Values [Pir00]*

Starting a debugging session, you never know in advance what exactly you'll learn. You seek lateral truths, as Robert M. Pirsig calls them. I intend to build upon the idea of lateral knowledge in this book. Foremost, I want to make sure you learn something about debugging web applications, but along the way, I'll be giving facts and ideas from other areas—philosophy, economics, linguistics, and history—when they feel relevant to the discussed matter in some wicked way. Just as lateral thinking, also known as thinking outside the box, comes to the rescue when analytical or "vertical" thinking falls short of the answer, learning outside the box strengthens the stem of knowledge and lets more branches of the learning tree grow. I hope you discover many more lateral truths both while you're reading this book and after. Happy debugging!

CHAPTER 1

Printing and Interpreting Errors

If you see an error, you're blessed. A good error message tells you what's gone wrong and helps you find where the problem is. A good error message has references to the line of code where it occurred, a call stack, and context—call parameters, OS and browser versions, and so on. Even if your error is not exceptional and misses details, it still will point you toward a starting point so you can figure out the rest.

In this chapter, we'll get you set up, and then we'll learn to interpret JavaScript errors and investigate them using an interactive debugger. We'll explore different error types.

To follow along, you need to know how to open the command line, how to browse developer tools, and how to switch between the JavaScript console and interactive debugger.

Setting Up for the Book

Chapter 3, Prioritizing Bugs, on page 29, and Chapter 4, Finding the Root Cause, on page 39, give foundational information and don't require a computer. But to get the most from the rest of this book, you should follow along with the exercises and install all the following software and tools, sorted from strictly necessary to optional:

- Chrome or another Chromium-based browser (Brave, Edge, Opera, Vivaldi). They all share the same platform: V8 as a JavaScript engine and Blink as a rendering engine.
- Visual Studio Code: a free and powerful open source text editor by Microsoft with plenty of useful extensions.
- Node.js, JavaScript runtime, and npm.

- Modern browsers based on engines other than Blink and V8:
  - Firefox, based on Gecko (rendering) and SpiderMonkey (JavaScript).
  - Safari, or Orion based on WebKit.

Mac, Linux, or Windows

You shouldn't have any trouble following this book using your platform of choice, with one notable exception—hotkeys. The key combinations in this book will be provided for the Mac. Most of the time, if you're using Linux or Windows, it's just a matter of pressing Ctrl where you read Cmd and Alt where you read Option. Sometimes, keyboard patterns have bigger differences, and I'll do my best to identify them whenever that turns out to be the case.

Chrome Developer Tools

We'll be using Google Chrome in this book, but feel free to use the browser of your choice. The developer tools will be mostly the same.

To open the JavaScript console in Chromium, press Options-Cmd-J or choose View > Developer > JavaScript Console in the top menu (as shown in the following image).

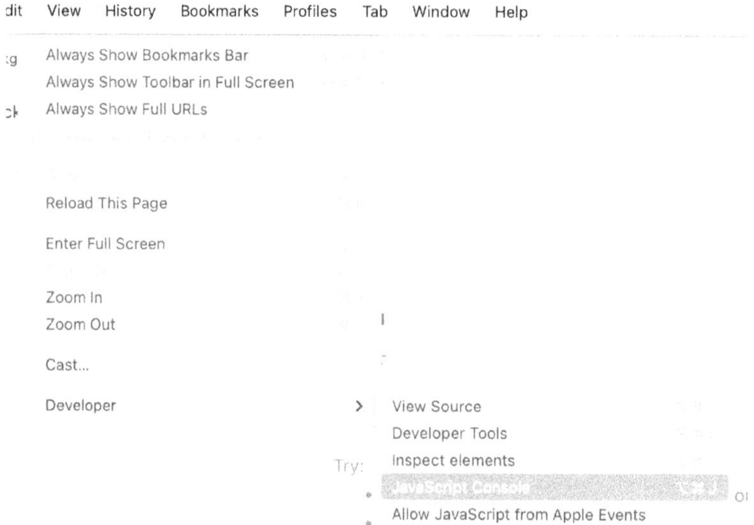

By default, Chrome developer tools open at the bottom of the screen. You can easily dock it to the right or left of the browser window, or even undock it to a separate window (which is especially convenient if you have a two-monitor setup).

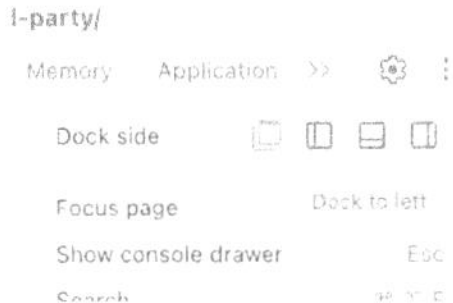

Changing the developer tools' size and position will adaptively change the position and visibility of UI panels, so your screen won't look the same as this book's images, but the difference is merely cosmetic.

On the top of the developer tools, you'll find tabs.

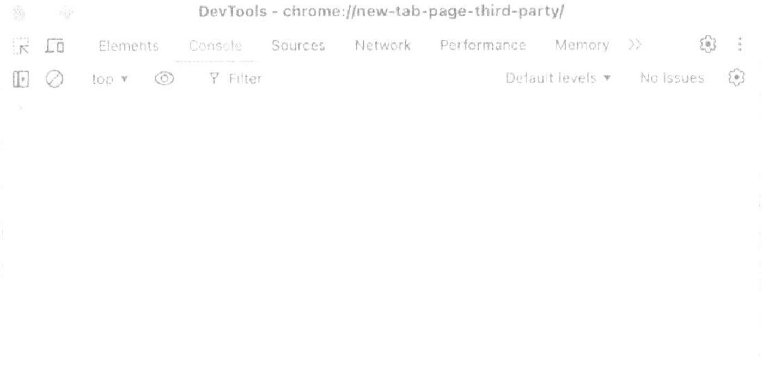

You can go directly to the element inspector by pressing Option-Command-C and opening wherever the developer tools panel was last opened by pressing Option-Command-I.

Installing VS Code and Extensions

The IDE used in this book is Visual Studio Code, which is open source and developed and maintained primarily by Microsoft. It can work with Git and TypeScript out of the box and lets you install plenty of third-party plug-ins from the marketplace: from C++ static analysis to project management tool integrations and AI-powered code companions. Note that the VS Code marketplace platform is controlled by Microsoft, and the binary, unlike the source code, has Microsoft telemetry built in.

We'll talk about setting up the developer infrastructure and productivity tools in Chapter 5, Designing Software That Doesn't Break, on page 53, but for now I'll list the plugins I recommend you install:

- ESLint
- Prettier
- Jest

If you don't like Visual Studio Code, you can use JetBrains WebStorm, which is free for noncommercial use and also has everything we need for this book out of the box.

Git and Repositories

This book's code samples are available on the PragProg website[1] and GitHub[2] for downloading. This book assumes that you have Git. You can follow the instructions on the Git website[3] to install it. Technically, you can work around Git by downloading .zip archives from GitHub instead of cloning repositories, but Git is the industry standard and it's good. Get it, really.

To clone a repository (download project files and the full history of changes to your local computer), you run `git clone`.

```
git clone https://github.com/oshibka404/xoxo.js.git
```

This command will clone a tic-tac-toe game written in JavaScript without external libraries or frameworks.

Node.js and npm Packages

Multiple ways of installing Node.js are available, depending on your operating system, preferred package manager, and habits. This book uses the one that works on both macOS and Linux. Go to nodejs.org, open the Download page, and enter the following in the terminal:

```
# installs nvm (Node Version Manager)
curl -o- https://raw.githubusercontent.com/nvm-sh/nvm/v0.40.1/install.sh | bash

# download and install Node.js (you may need to restart the terminal)
nvm install 24
```

This book uses Node v24.11, which is the most current LTS (long-time support) version. If you have another version of Node.js, you can and should use the node version manager to switch between versions. This book uses `nvm`, the most used of the alternatives at the time of this writing.

```
# to use the version we use in the book
nvm use 24
```

If you've switched to a different version, you can go back to the latest LTS version by running this:

```
nvm use --lts
```

1. https://pragprog.com/titles/aodjs/
2. https://github.com
3. https://git-scm.com/downloads

This book uses node.js tools, such as package manager Yarn, test runner Jest, and static analyzer ESLint. We'll also use Frameworks and libraries such as React, Lodash, and Astro. To install these packages from npm, use the following:

```
# Install Jest and save to developer dependencies
npm install jest --save-dev

# install React and save it to project dependencies
npm install react

# install a specific version of lodash (in this example, v3)
npm install lodash@3

# Install yarn and make it available globally
npm install --global yarn

# After installing a package globally, you can call it in command line directly:
yarn
```

Alternatives

This book mostly uses tools such as Node, NVM, npm, ESLint, and Git, which are mature and widespread enough to not cease to exist in next couple of years. Still, alternatives exist that are in general faster, provide a better developer experience, or are based on a different paradigm. All of them are worth trying or reading about.

Command-line tools and npm packages include the following:

- Node.js: bun, deno
- NVM: fnm
- npm: yarn, pnpm or, again, bun
- ESLint: Biome
- Git: jj
- Jest: vitest

Web tools and desktop software include the following:

- GitHub: CodeBerg
- VS Code: WebStorm

Checklist

Once you have the following installed, you're good to go:

- Chrome or another Chromium-based browser
- Visual Studio Code
- Node.js and npm
- Git

If you choose to use alternative software while following this book, I assume you know what you're doing or are willing to do some research on your own. Now that everything's ready, you can start having some fun.

Getting Started with Debugging

We'll start with debugging a production website rather than a locally running copy where you have full edit access to all the files. In the usual debugging process, this is the first step after a bug is reported by an external user: you open the same URL as they did and try to get the same results as they did. After you've managed to reproduce the problem, you start exploring to find the boundaries of the bug: Does the same thing happen on other pages? Does it happen on a local copy? On refresh? In a different browser? On a different OS? With another screen resolution? With a different zoom level?

A good bug reproduction has many nuances, as does a good bug report, and we'll talk about them in depth in Chapter 4, Finding the Root Cause, on page 39. But first things first. We'll start investigating an easily reproduced error on a remote site using only a browser.

Fixing Common Errors

Open the tic-tac-toe game page[4] in a browser. The page opens and the playing field is visible, but nothing happens when you click. Let's fix it.

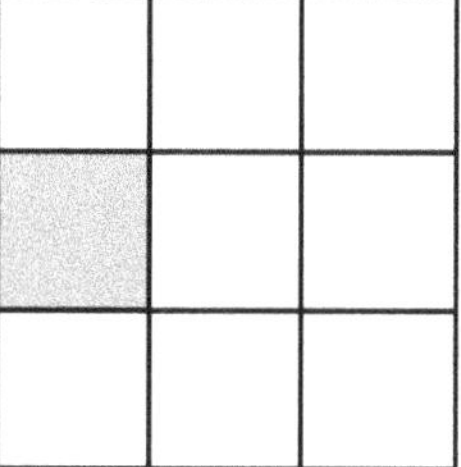

Fixing a SyntaxError with Code Overrides

Open the JavaScript console and you'll see `Uncaught SyntaxError: Unexpected token '{'` written in red. `SyntaxError`, of all the error types, is the easiest to deal with. Usually it means that you need to add or remove one character. As shown in the following image, right next to it, you'll see a clickable link to the line and column where JavaScript parsing failed.

4. https://oshibka404.github.io/xoxo.js/

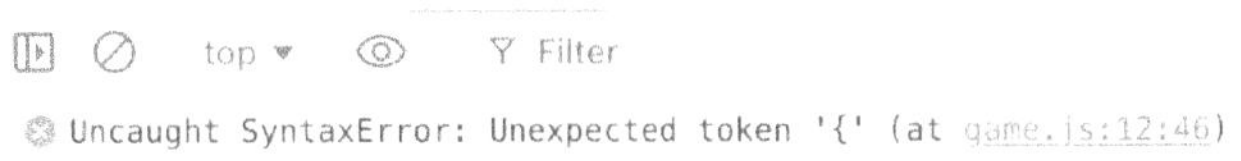

```
Uncaught SyntaxError: Unexpected token '{' (at game.js:12:46)
```

Clicking it will show you a code listing with the suspected line highlighted (see the next image).

```
}
                                        Uncaught SyntaxError: Unexpected token '{'
document.getElementById("game").addEventListe...
    if (e.target.classList.contains("clear") {
        e.target.classList.replace("clear", state.currentPlayer)
        state.currentPlayer = state.currentPlayer === "x" ? "o" : "x"
        state.winner = checkWinner()
        if (state.winner) {
```

If the syntax mistake is not immediately clear from there, this would be the typical sequence of actions to find it:

1. Count the opening and closing brackets of each kind around the error origin. (For example, { ([ ] } is missing a closing) bracket.)
2. Check that the order of closing brackets matches the order of the opening ones. (For example, ({ }) is valid, but ({) } is not.)
3. Check commas, colons, and semicolons. (For example, the declaration `function foo(a b)` misses a `,` between its arguments. It should be `function foo(a, b)`.)
4. Google the error text, having removed variable names and values from it.

In our case, the `if` condition is missing the closing parenthesis). Note that `Unexpected token "{"` does not always mean that the { shouldn't be there. Often it means that something that the code parser failed to find there should exist before it.

SyntaxError in Other Browsers

The JavaScript engine of WebKit-based browsers like Safari and Orion has an even more detailed description of `SyntaxError` than Chrome's V8. It not only tells you what unexpected character breaks the code parsing but also points out which character is expected, making the fix even easier for you. In our example, it would leave less ambiguity and print the following:

```
SyntaxError: Unexpected token '{'. Expected ')' to end an 'if' condition.
```

SpiderMonkey, the JavaScript engine of Firefox, provides a handy link called "[Learn More]" that leads to the MDN page with a description and common causes of this specific error:

```
Uncaught SyntaxError: missing ) after condition [Learn More]    game.js:12:46
```

If we were debugging a page in local files, we'd open the game.js file in a code editor, add the missing), save the file, and refresh the page in the browser. But we're debugging a remote web page with its source code on a server where we cannot easily upload a new version of a file and check whether it works. We'll have to use local files on remote sites, and Chromium-based browsers allow us to do that using local overrides.

Local Overrides

In the Sources tab, add the missing parenthesis, then right-click the code editor and select Override Content.

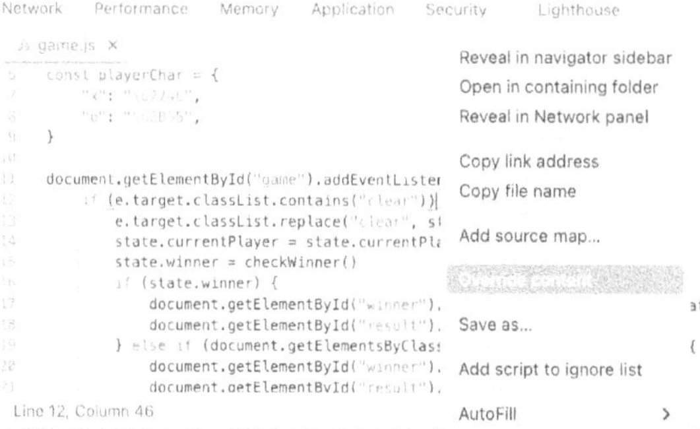

The browser will ask you to choose a folder to store the override files in (which can be any folder) and permit it to access the folder. Now refresh the page, click any of the cells, and enjoy that the error is gone.

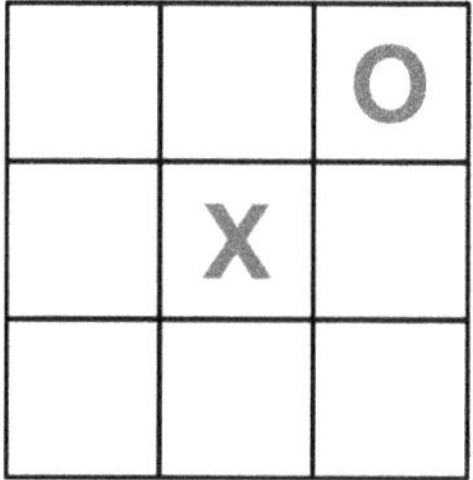

From now on, you can access your local overrides in the left sidebar of the Sources panel, in the Overrides tab. Going forward, all the style changes you make on the pages of this website will also be preserved between sessions, unless you explicitly disable this functionality or uncheck the Enable Local Overrides checkbox (see the following image).

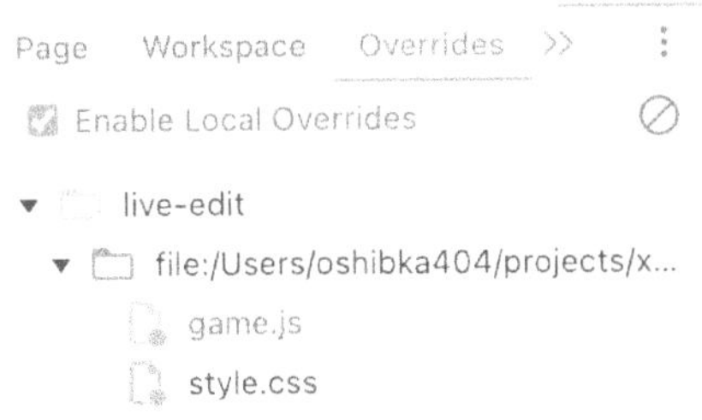

SyntaxErrors are not only the easiest errors to fix but also the easiest to prevent. Visual Studio Code, WebStorm, Zed, or any other modern web-oriented text editor will highlight these errors in no time. Sometimes, for various reasons, you might have to edit the code in web editors, using automated scripts, or in the console without the syntax highlighted, so the code editors won't help. If it happens often enough for the problem to be noticeable, you can set up a Git hook validating code on commit and set up continuous integration (CI).

Syntax errors will be many times easier to find if you practice consistent formatting, and automation will help too. Use Prettier[5] or Biome[6] to validate or even autofix code formatting. It's helpful when you're on your own, and it's essential in a large team. We'll discuss developer infrastructure in more detail in Chapter 5, Designing Software That Doesn't Break, on page 53.

Fixing TypeError with Interactive Debugging

If you're from this planet and have played tic-tac-toe before, you'll quickly notice that our game doesn't work. In a real tic-tac-toe game, when one of the players gets three crosses or circles in a row, column, or diagonal, the player wins and the game is supposed to finish. On our page, that doesn't happen, and the losing player can make moves even after being beaten, as you can see in the following image.

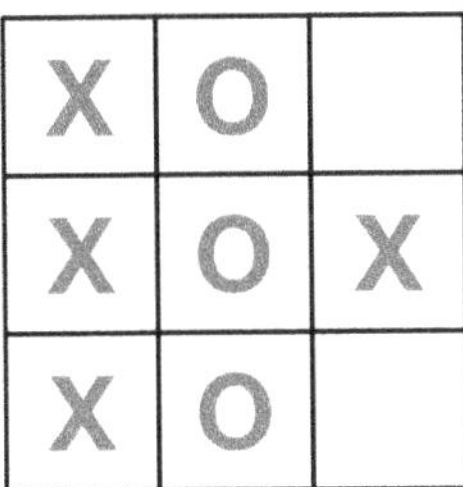

5. https://prettier.io/
6. https://biomejs.dev/

To start investigating why, let's take another look in the JavaScript console. You'll find two unique error messages:

```
▸ Uncaught ReferenceError: Cannot access 'reset' before initialization
    at game.js:26:62
▸ Uncaught TypeError: document.getElementsByTagName(...).map is not a function
    at checkWinner (game.js:38:55)
    at HTMLTableElement.<anonymous> (game.js:15:24)
```

Let's investigate the error using interactive debugging, a powerful technique that we'll be using a lot in this book and will dive deep into in Chapter 6, Following the Data Flow, on page 77. With the page open, go to the Sources tab and enable the Pause on Uncaught Exceptions checkmark.

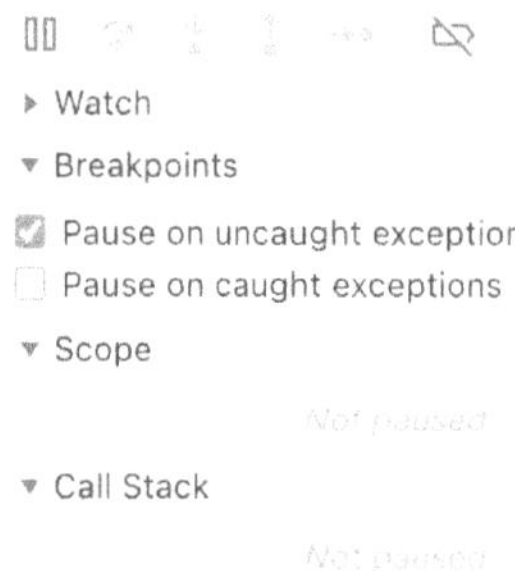

Click a game cell to make a move. The execution pauses on the line where the error is happening, and the code listing automatically scrolls to that line. Now you have access to all the values of variables and properties that are in the visible area of the line and column where the exception is thrown. Hover over the cells variable. In the pop-up, you see that cells is an instance of HTMLCollection and has indexed properties that we are unsuccessfully trying to iterate through using map:

```
Sources   Network   Performance
game.js   style.        HTMLCollection(9)
document.getElement     ▸ 0: td.x
                        ▸ 1: td.clear
const reset = () =>     ▸ 2: td.clear
    state.winner =      ▸ 3: td.clear
    state.currentPl     ▸ 4: td.clear
    for (const cell     ▸ 5: td.clear
        cell.classN     ▸ 6: td.clear
    }                   ▸ 7: td.clear
    document.getEle     ▸ 8: td.clear
}                         length: 9
                        ▾ : HTMLCollection
function checkWinne       ▸ item: f item()
                            length: (...)
                          ▸ namedItem: f namedItem()
    const cells = document.getElementsByTagName(...)
    const squares = cells.map(({className}) => className === "cle
    const lines = [
        [0, 1, 2],
{ } Line 39, Column 27
```

If you expand prototype to see what methods of HTMLCollection are available, you'll see that there is indeed no method called map. Multiple options exist to map a collection of cells to an array of "x", "o", and "", depending on the cell class.

For example, you can rewrite the method to use for... of instead of map to iterate across all items or transform the HTMLCollection into an array and keep the rest of the logic as it is. Let's do the latter and replace cells.map with [...cells].map. HTMLCollection allows us to do this because it's an Iterable, which we can tell because it has a [[Symbol.Iterator]] in the prototype.

```
[...cells].map(({className}) => className === "clear" ? "" : className)
```

Edit and press Cmd+S to save the override, then refresh the page. Verify that the proper winner check works now.

TypeErrors can sometimes be tricky to track, but you can prevent them with technical measures, the best kind of prevention. Switch to TypeScript and don't circumvent its restrictions; they're there for a reason. We'll talk more about using and configuring TypeScript for your projects in Chapter 5, Designing Software That Doesn't Break, on page 53.

Fixing ReferenceError by Moving Code Blocks

The Restart button doesn't work. If you follow the same steps as we did earlier (either click the link in the JavaScript console or pause on exception and refresh the page), you'll see that reset is not defined yet when it's being called.

Two schools of thought exist regarding Method ordering. One encourages the main procedure of a module, or an entry point, to be placed on top with all of its subroutines declared below, in order of appearance. The other perspective prescribes every function in the module to be declared before it's referenced. Either approach is possible for this case. Whichever approach you choose, be consistent (at least within a single project), especially if you're not working alone. Following a rule consistently often matters more than whatever the rule actually is.

These are your options to fix the error:

1. Change the function expression to the function declaration: replace const reset = () => { with function reset() {. Function declarations rise to the top of their scope and can be safely referenced from there.
2. Take the function as it is and move it above its usage.

On the Importance of Naming

Even without interactive debugging, it's often possible to figure out where to start investigating just by carefully reading the errors. In our case we have two errors: ReferenceError mentions something about reset, which might be relevant somehow, but the TypeError has a checkWinner function in its call stack, and we know that there's a problem somewhere around checking whether there's a winner. If the function were named not checkWinner but doThings, we wouldn't have such an advantage.

Pick either option, save the file by pressing Cmd+S, and refresh the page.

Both actions can have side effects that are not relevant in this scenario but in many cases will be. Arrow functions, declared with the syntax () => {}, preserve the context where they're declared, whereas functions using the keyword function will use the context of the call. Be aware that if you change a function with this used in its body from an arrow function to a class method or vice versa, you're likely to break something.

Another important consideration is that execution order matters a lot, and if to fix a ReferenceError you do something more significant than swapping a function and a reference to it, double-check that the other code in the module doesn't rely on it being where it was.

That being said, congratulations! The tic-tac-toe game works. If you cloned the repository, you can copy the fixed file contents to the text editor, open index.html in a browser, and play around with the code.

Looking Up Errors

Many other error types exist—RangeError, URIError, AggregateError—and dozens of different TypeErrors and SyntaxErrors. They all have lots in common within each type, and the techniques we learned in this chapter will help you to deal with any of them.

When you google the error, remember to delete your data and names of your variables from the request. Having them will only worsen the search result quality.

AI tools can be useful in interpreting and mitigating errors, but the burden of validation and the final judgment stays with you, the human. It's perfectly fine to apply a fix suggested by AI, but make sure you understand well how the fix works; otherwise, you can't be sure that it's a good fix. "If you didn't fix it, it ain't fixed." What's more, if you end up breaking it worse, it needs to be fixed even more.

Mozilla Developer Network has a great JavaScript Error Reference[7] page listing all existing native JavaScript errors, their versions in different families of browsers, common causes, and solutions to them.

Wrapping Up

Now that you've completed this chapter, you're able to trace the program execution flow by printing console messages without interrupting it. You can pause the program execution, inspect its state, and resume, using the interactive debugger. You're also able to interpret JavaScript errors you see in the console.

In the next chapter, we'll use this knowledge of errors and logging to build reliable, easily debuggable software systems.

7. https://developer.mozilla.org/en-US/docs/Web/JavaScript/Reference/Errors

CHAPTER 2

Setting Guardrails with Throw and Catch

"Cat the, also." "Along find big." These sentences are meaningless because the words don't work in their positions, and it's easy to spot even without trying to understand their meaning. On the other hand, "Grass eats cow" and "Cold water burns" are both grammatically correct, but they also make little sense, unless you're into psychedelic poetry. To catch this mistake, you'll have to try to draw a picture in your mind and realize that it doesn't match the reality. Things become more complex when you have a longer text. "Michael was born in 1954. His parents met each other at a Beatles concert." Each sentence in isolation is fine and passes the plausibility check, but combined, they can't be factually correct: The Beatles didn't exist in 1954, and a person couldn't be born before his parents met. The longer your text is, the more entities interact in it, and the more likely it is for you to overlook such a contradiction.

A computer has no idea what your program intends to do. It receives commands and executes them in a deterministic and predictable manner. This is what makes computers such powerful tools, but it also demands full responsibility for the result from the programmer. You have to give the right commands and provide the right data to get the right results. The creators of the language infrastructure have created many great tools to help you with that responsibility: garbage collectors handle memory cleanup, and other tools check syntax and do static analysis.

All the errors we discussed in the previous chapter serve the same purpose of catching potential bugs before they can ruin the user experience. The language itself is helping the programmer avoid common mistakes. But here's bad news for you—a language on its own can automatically catch only language-level mistakes. Solution-level mistakes, let alone problem-level mistakes, lie in the domain of human intention, and if you want a computer to catch them, you'll have to intentionally program it to do so. Let's talk about how. We'll cover how to throw and catch errors. By the end of the chapter we'll write a small library that will create an object wrapper that logs all operations.

Fail-Fast and Fault-Tolerant Systems

When it comes to building reliable systems, there are two complementary strategies that might sound mutually exclusive at first. One (fail fast) is to detect values that are logically impossible, but technically possible due to a bug, and forcefully stop execution—such as by showing an error screen. The other (fault tolerant) is to knowingly let the error happen, silently ensuring it causes no damage, and let the rest of the program run as if nothing happened. Most real-world software combines both approaches, and you as a software designer will use your own judgment to find a good balance between the two.

Forcefully stopping the execution flow is called throwing an exception and is done using the `throw` statement followed by an expression to be thrown.

```
function formatName(name) {
    if (typeof name !== "string") {
        throw "name is not a string";
    }

    if (name.length === 0) {
        throw "the name is empty";
    }

    return name.toLowerCase().capitalize();
}
```

In the preceding example, the function will return a formatted name only if the argument is a string and it's not empty. Otherwise, it will interrupt the execution flow and throw an exception.

Handling an exception, no matter if thrown by a developer or by the JavaScript runtime, can be done using a `try...catch` statement:

```
let name

try {
    const input = document.getElementById("name");
    name = formatName(input.value);
} catch (error) {
    name = "Joe";
    console.error(error);
}

console.info(`The name is ${name}`)
```

In this example, if an element with ID "name" is not found on the page, the input will be null, and an attempt to access its value property will throw an exception. Also, if the element is found but is not an input, thus doesn't have the value property, or if it's an empty input, the function formatName will throw an exception. However, when these exceptions occur in a try block, the catch block will be executed with the exception passed to it as an argument. We'll assign a default name and print the error in the console. The program will keep running.

Let's discuss how to use throw and catch in practice to build fail-fast and fault-tolerant systems.

Building a Fail-Fast System

Eliminating bugs is ideal, but transforming them from critical to major or from major to minor is preferable to doing nothing, and users will be grateful if you unblock their work, even if it means that something else will look incomplete. During development, intentionally blocking code paths that could lead to data corruption is a good move, even if it blocks a major user flow or crashes the whole app. The same is true if you unblock a critical flow at the cost of knowingly breaking a less important feature.

Fail-fast systems prefer to halt execution whenever a code path may corrupt the data. Usually, the more critical a subsystem is, the more it makes sense to make it fail fast. For example, in a bank application, the code paths that are rounding numbers should have a lot of checks and throw an exception whenever an error occurs, but the paths setting smooth animations don't have to.

```
function average(numbers: number[]) {
    if (numbers.length === 0) throw Error("The list cannot be empty")

    const sum = numbers.reduce((acc, num) => acc + num, 0)
    return sum / numbers.length
}
```

This way, you don't let nonsense happen (like returning Infinity), and the function doesn't silently swallow the error but instead throws an exception you can catch and handle. Let's write a small benchmarking utility using this averaging function to smooth out the measurement fluctuations. It will accept a function, run it a set number of times, and print out the average running time of the function.

```
const result = document.getElementById("result")

function benchmark(func: () => void, runCount: number): void {
    const measurements: number[] = []
```

```
    for (let i = 0; i < runCount; i++) {
        const start = performance.now()
        func()
        measurements.push(performance.now() - start)
    }
    const runningTime = average(measurements)
    result.innerText = `The function takes on average
     ${runningTime} from ${runCount} runs.`
}
```

Now, if the measurement count happens to be `0`, we'll throw an exception instead of displaying `Infinity`, and if the measured function `func` itself throws, the exception will be passed up the call stack. However, if you don't handle the thrown exception, the user won't see anything. They'll assume the program isn't working. An easy way to make it visible would be to wrap the entry point in `try` and show the user a message in `catch`:

```
try {
    const runCount = document.getElementById("run-count").valueAsNumber
    benchmark(longOperation, runCount)
} catch (error) {
    alert(error.message)
}
```

This code, in addition to halting a potentially malicious and confusing behavior, informs the user of the error. In the real world, instead of calling `alert`, which is very aggressive, it's more common to show an on-page error notification (for example, `statusEl.innerHtml = error.message`) or alter the style of a UI element (say, `inputEl.style.borderColor = "red"`). The point is to be explicit when something goes wrong (the value is not valid) and suggest what the user can do about it (use a positive value).

Building a Fault-Tolerant System

Not every subsystem is so important that preventing its misbehavior is worth halting the bigger system. Or, to reframe the same thought, some systems are critical enough that a failure of one of its parts shouldn't block the whole system from running.

If your program is a railroad network, you want to emergency stop a train if you notice the possibility of a crash, even if you have to stop all trains nearby as well. But if you stop all trains in one part of the country, you want to make sure that the trains in other areas keep going. This is what we call *graceful degradation.* On top of that, if you calculate a safe alternative route for every train in the dangerous area, you can send the trains there, thus leaving your transport connection uninterrupted. This is what we call *fault tolerance.*

For example, to turn our previous example from fail fast into a graceful degradation, we can swap alert for console.log, so that it won't interrupt behavior and the program will keep running:

```
try {
    benchmark(longOperation, runCount)
} catch (error) {
    console.error(error.message)
}
```

To turn this example into fault tolerant, we could, for example, retry calling benchmark with an appropriate default number of counts:

```
const DEFAULT_SAMPLE_COUNT = 128
try {
    benchmark(longOperation, runCount)
} catch (error) {
    console.error(`Error: ${error.message}, retrying...`)
    benchmark(longOperation, DEFAULT_SAMPLE_COUNT)
}
```

Note that this example does not account for all other possible errors. To make a truly fault-tolerant system, you need to have a plan B for everything that could possibly go wrong.

What graceful degradation and fault tolerance have in common is the notion that faults are inevitable and the whole system shall keep on running despite them. They both require a notion of what parts can fail and in what way. Graceful degradation can be achieved by loose coupling: isolating modules and making them independent of one another. Fault tolerance is achieved by recovery tactics such as retry, replication, and failure-oblivious computing.

System reliability is a big topic of its own, with many great books on it. A couple of these are *Site Reliability Engineering*[1] and *Building Secure and Reliable Systems*.[2] At the risk of oversimplification, here's some brief guidance on when to use each approach:

- Use fail fast during development to catch issues early.
- Use fail fast for critical parts where not functioning at all is preferable to functioning wrong (for example, risk of data corruption or misleading the user).
- Use graceful degradation for noncritical features to ensure a smooth user experience during partial failures.

1. https://www.oreilly.com/library/view/site-reliability-engineering/9781491929117/
2. https://www.oreilly.com/library/view/building-secure-and/9781492083115/

- Use fault tolerance for core modules that must remain fully operational for the whole system to work.

We'll discuss both graceful degradation and fault tolerance in more detail in Chapter 5, Designing Software That Doesn't Break, on page 53. No matter which approach you take, you should log every fault. Let's talk about logging techniques beyond console.log.

Advanced Logging

Logs are your main tool for nondisruptive debugging. The program will keep executing normally but leave the message trail for you to read and analyze. console.log is the most neutral way of printing text in a console. Its siblings are console.warn, console.error, and console.info; they're mostly the same with built-in styles, and the only significant practical difference between them is that you can filter by message level to see, say, only errors or only warnings and info messages, as shown in the following image.

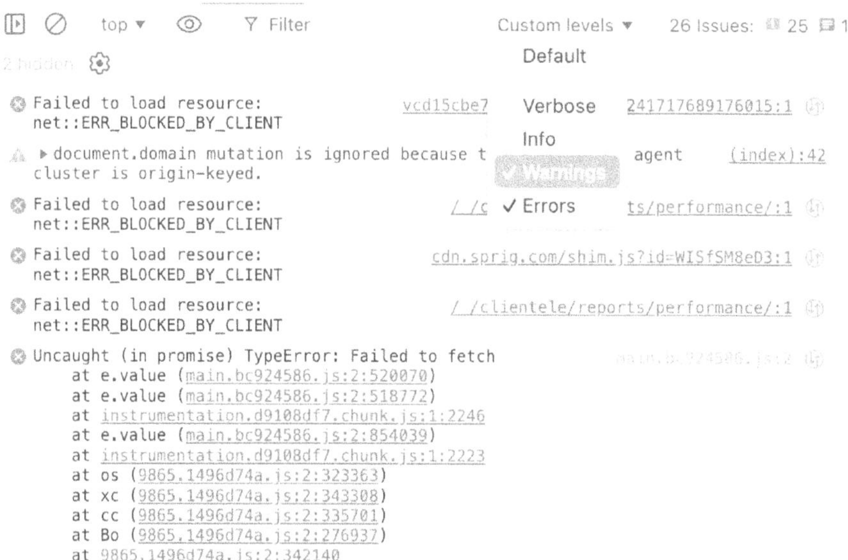

The output of console.debug looks the same as log and is one level lower than info, and in Chrome DevTools it corresponds to the Verbose log level.

Despite the fact that console.error looks like the result of throwing an uncaught exception, it will not break the execution flow and your program will keep running. A useful alternative to console.error is console.assert: it prints the error only if its first argument is evaluated to false; otherwise it does nothing.

By default, the console will be cleared on page refresh, but you can disable it by switching on Preserve Log in console settings, as shown in the next image.

It's useful when troubleshooting a page loading or a bug not consistently reproduced on every session.

When you throw an instance of `Error`, the printed output will contain the stack trace, which helps enormously, but if you want to log the trace without interrupting the execution, use `console.trace`. It's extremely useful when debugging a utility function with side effects. If such a function is being called from different contexts and produces wrong results only in some of them, `console.trace` lets you contextualize each call by matching it with the caller, and the caller's caller, and so on. Another situation when you might need `console.trace` is when the order of calls to the same function matters. A whole big category of bugs is caused by race condition or, to put it more simply, wrong execution order of asynchronous operations.

When the correct count of calls matters more than the order, `console.count` comes in handy. In addition to the message, it shows the number of calls with each particular message. To reset to 0, call `console.countReset` with the message you want to reset:

```
console.count("A") // 1
console.count("A") // 2
console.count("B") // 1
console.count("A") // 3
console.count("B") // 2
console.countReset("A") // resetting counter for "A" back to 0
console.count("A") // 1
console.count("B") // 3
```

Printing Structured Data

Two common data structures you'll encounter in any application are trees and tables. A table is typically represented as a flat array of "row" objects with identical fields. `console.table` is the perfect tool to print such a structure.

```
const people = [
    {name: 'Andrey', job: 'Programmer'},
    {name: 'Daria', job: 'Architect'},
    {name: 'Max', job: 'Engineer'},
]

console.table(people)
```

The table printed in the console as a result (shown in the following image) is not only formatted but also sortable by any column.

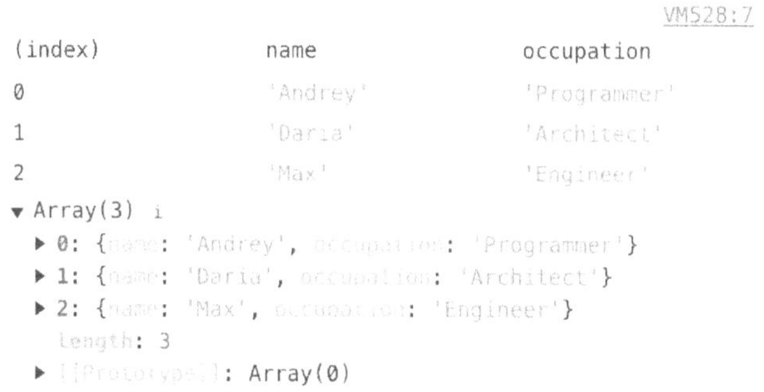

```
                                                  VM528:7
(index)            name               occupation
0                  'Andrey'           'Programmer'
1                  'Daria'            'Architect'
2                  'Max'              'Engineer'
▼ Array(3) i
  ▶ 0: {name: 'Andrey', occupation: 'Programmer'}
  ▶ 1: {name: 'Daria', occupation: 'Architect'}
  ▶ 2: {name: 'Max', occupation: 'Engineer'}
    length: 3
  ▶ [[Prototype]]: Array(0)
```

console.table will not be of much help if you want to print data that doesn't fit a table well—for example, a tree, a graph, or a configuration object with deep nesting. The most generic way of printing an object is console.dir. It prints an expandable hierarchy of object properties, as the following image shows.

```
> console.dir(window.location)
  ▼ Location i                                          VM151:1
    ▶ ancestorOrigins: DOMStringList {length: 0}
    ▶ assign: ƒ assign()
      hash: ""
      host: "duckduckgo.com"
      hostname: "duckduckgo.com"
      href: "https://duckduckgo.com/chrome_newtab"
      origin: "https://duckduckgo.com"
      pathname: "/chrome_newtab"
      port: ""
      protocol: "https:"
    ▶ reload: ƒ reload()
    ▶ replace: ƒ replace()
      search: ""
    ▶ toString: ƒ toString()
    ▶ valueOf: ƒ valueOf()
      Symbol(Symbol.toPrimitive):
    ▶ [[Prototype]]: Location
```

The output of console.dir always represents the JavaScript properties available at the runtime. console.log and most other printing methods will alter their output format depending on the object class, but console.dir is predictable, as shown in the following two screenshots.

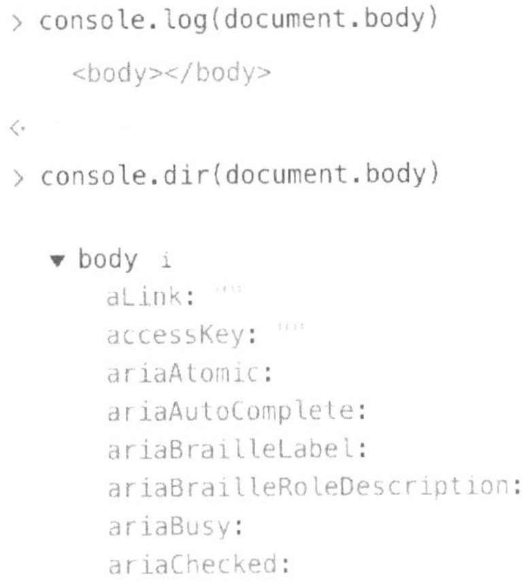

```
> console.log(document.body)
    <body></body>
<·
> console.dir(document.body)

  ▼ body i
      aLink: ""
      accessKey: ""
      ariaAtomic:
      ariaAutoComplete:
      ariaBrailleLabel:
      ariaBrailleRoleDescription:
      ariaBusy:
      ariaChecked:
```

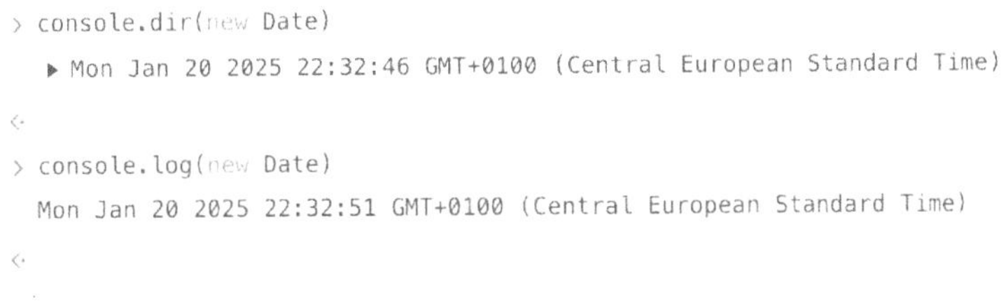

```
> console.dir(new Date)
  ▶ Mon Jan 20 2025 22:32:46 GMT+0100 (Central European Standard Time)
<·
> console.log(new Date)
  Mon Jan 20 2025 22:32:51 GMT+0100 (Central European Standard Time)
<·
```

Hierarchical data structures may contain data not interesting to you during debugging. If you want to log only the ID of each tree node and be able to collapse and expand each level, you can do it using console.group, console.groupCollapsed, and console.groupEnd. Use console.group to print an initially expanded group and console.groupCollapsed for a collapsed group.

```
type TreeNode = {
    title: string
    children: TreeNode[]
}

function printTree(node: TreeNode) {
    if (node.children.length === 0) {
        console.log(node.title)
    } else {
        console.group(node.title)
        node.children.forEach((child) => {
            printTree(child)
        })
        console.groupEnd()
    }
}
```

Every call to console.group or console.groupCollapsed will increase the nesting level of the following output, and every call to console.groupEnd will decrease it by one. This method of structural data logging requires more manual work but gives you full control over what's being printed or left out.

String Substitutions

You can have even more control over output by applying string substitutions. Let's write a utility function creating a proxy for a given function that will log every access to its property:

```
function createFunctionLogger(func: Function) {
    return new Proxy(func, {
        apply: function(target, context, argumentsList) {
            const result = target.apply(context, argumentsList)
            console.log(
                "Calling function %s with arguments %O.",
                target.name,
                argumentsList,
                "Return value is %o"
                result
            )
            return result
        }
    })
}
```

We used %s here to print the property name as a string and %O to print arguments as generic JS objects—essentially, an inline version of console.dir. But more curious here is %o, which we used to print return values. The console inlines them formatted in an optimal way, depending on their type: for instance, plain objects will be presented as expandable trees, DOM elements will look like they would in Web Inspector, strings will remain strings, and so on.

Additionally, there are three special string substitutions to insert numeric values: %d and its equivalent %i format value as an integer, and %f formats it as a floating point number. If a string or an object is passed for substitution, it will be rendered as NaN.

Let's build an object logger with an access counter to each property:

```
function createObjectLogger<T extends object>(obj: T): T {
    const accessCounter = new Map<string, number>()

    return new Proxy(obj, {
        get: function(target: T, prop: string | symbol) {
            const value = Reflect.get(target, prop)
            if (value instanceof Function) {
```

```
                return createFunctionLogger(value)
            }
            const accessCount = (accessCounter.get(prop) ?? 0) + 1
            accessCounter.set(prop, accessCount)
            console.log(
                "Accessing property %s (%d), its value is %o",
                prop,
                accessCount,
                value
            )
            return value
        },
        set: function(target: T, prop: string | symbol, value: unknown) {
            console.log(`Setting property %s to %o`, prop, value)
            Reflect.set(target, prop, value)
            return true
        },
    })
}
function createFunctionLogger(func: Function) {
    // same as in previous example
}
```

The output of this proxy is already very informative, but we can do better. Let's make it prettier and more readable by applying styles.

Styling Console Messages

%c is another string substitution that will apply CSS style rules to the rest of the string that comes after it.

```
const groupStyle = `
    display: inline-block;
    cursor: pointer;
    padding: 4px;
    border-radius: 4px;
    color: #fff;
    background-color: #33c;
`
const messageStyle = "color: #eee; background-color: #333;"

console.groupCollapsed("%cExpand me", groupStyle)
console.log("%cMessage in a group", messageStyle)
console.groupEnd()
```

Expand me

Message in a group

You can apply several style sets within the same string. Note that every consecutive style set will fully replace the previous one rather than override it. So if you first apply a text color and then apply only background, the color will be reset to default, and vice versa. By applying an empty style set, you'll reset the following text to the default style:

```
console.log(
    "This %cmessage %chas%c multiple %cstyles",
    "color: #f33",
    "background-color: #fcc",
    "color: #3f3",
    ""
);
```

```
This message has          styles
```

Different browsers support slightly different lists of CSS properties for console messages—for instance, Firefox supports cursor while Chrome and Safari don't. Here's a non-comprehensive list of CSS properties supported in all major browsers:

- background and its longhand equivalents
- border and its longhand equivalents
- border-radius
- box-shadow
- color
- display
- font and its longhand equivalents
- line-height
- margin
- outline and its longhand equivalents
- padding
- text-* properties such as text-decoration
- white-space
- word-spacing and word-break

Taking it all into account, let's improve the styles of the logged method:

```
const getterStyle = 'color: #3f3;'
const setterStyle = 'color: #f33;'
const callStyle = 'color: #33f;'
const counterStyle = `
    color: white;
    background-color: #333;
    display: inline-block;
    padding: 4px;
```

```
    border-radius: 4px;
`

function createObjectLogger<T extends object>(obj: T): T {
    const accessCounter = new Map<string, number>()

    return new Proxy(obj, {
        get: function(target: T, prop: string) {
            const value = Reflect.get(target, prop)
            if (value instanceof Function) {
                return createFunctionLogger(value)
            }
            const accessCount = (accessCounter.get(prop) ?? 0) + 1
            accessCounter.set(prop, accessCount)
            console.log(
                "%cAccessing property %c%s %c%d%c, its value is %o",
                getterStyle,
                "",
                prop,
                counterStyle,
                accessCount,
                "",
                value)
            return value
        },
        set: function(target, prop, value) {
            console.log(
                "%cSetting property %c%s%c to %o",
                setterStyle,
                "",
                prop,
                "",
                value
            )
            Reflect.set(target, prop, value)
            return true
        },
    })
}

function createFunctionLogger(func: Function) {
    return new Proxy(func, {
        apply: function(target, context, argumentsList) {
            const result = target.apply(context, argumentsList)
            console.log(
                "%cCalling function %c%s%c with arguments %O.",
                callStyle,
                "",
                target.name,
                "",
                argumentsList,
                "Return value is %o",
```

```
                result
            )
            return result
        }
    })
}
```

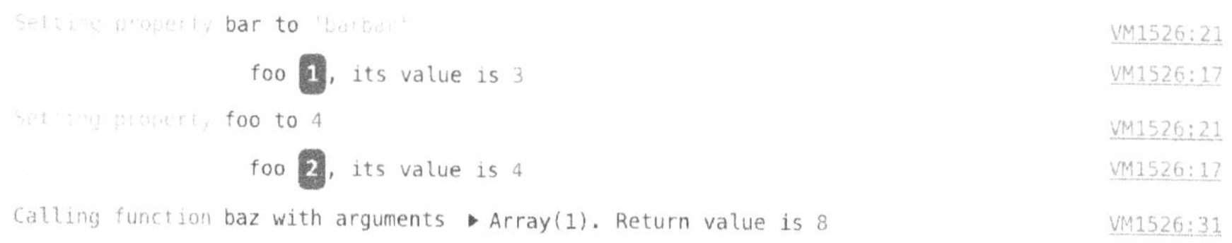

```
Setting property bar to 'barbar'                                  VM1526:21
                foo 1, its value is 3                             VM1526:17
Setting property foo to 4                                         VM1526:21
                foo 2, its value is 4                             VM1526:17
Calling function baz with arguments ▶ Array(1). Return value is 8 VM1526:31
```

In the preceding image, read operations are green, method invocations are blue, and write operations are logged in red, so visually distinguishing them will be easy for you.

You might have noticed in these examples that a log call with multiple substitutions quickly gets messy, so try to keep your log messages short and concise. Ideally, one log record should correspond to one piece of information. Misleading logs can be worse than no logs at all.

Wrapping Up

You're now able to throw and catch exceptions. You know the difference between fail-fast and fault-tolerant systems and can identify when to choose one over the other. You know how to create wrappers logging access to object members and how to style the console output.

In the next chapter, we'll cover how to pick the most impactful bugs to work on and balance them against other product work.

CHAPTER 3

Prioritizing Bugs

"It is the greatest happiness of the greatest number that is the measure of right and wrong," wrote Jeremy Bentham, the creator of utilitarian philosophy, in 1776. Though arguable, it's a great principle to keep in mind while prioritizing your work. Your product helps people solve problems. Some problems are bigger than others, and some problems concern more people than others. Some problems are easy to solve, while others will take ages, and you have only so much time. Use it wisely.

When choosing what to work on, you want to prioritize:

- the worst of the issues,
- concerning the most people,
- that's the fastest to solve.

It's rare for all three factors to point to the same issue at the same time; otherwise, you wouldn't have to ever worry about priorities. In reality, you'll have to find a balance between the three.

In this chapter, we'll cover how to determine bug severity, reach, and fix time. Then we'll talk about timeboxing and three-point estimation and learn to quantify bug priority using the RICE technique.

Estimating Bug Severity

It's common to segregate bugs into buckets by their severity and priority. To put it bluntly, severity is how bad the life of the user is, and priority is how strongly we need to do something about it relative to other tasks. Three severity buckets that you'll find almost everywhere are Critical, Major, and Minor. Sometimes teams will increase the bucket count by adding Blocker above Critical, Medium between Major and Minor, and Low, aka Trivial, below Minor.

To put it in familiar terms, let's take as an example a typical video call application similar to Zoom, Around, or Google Meet. The examples of bugs on each severity level could be these:

1. *Minor:* A visual defect or a broken optional feature. For example, icons or emoji reactions don't work. It's nice and fun to have them, but if not, no one's work is going to be interrupted because of that, no money is lost, and no workflow is broken.

2. *Major:* Important functionality is broken. For instance, users cannot send text messages in the meeting chat.

3. *Critical:* A critical flow is blocked. Users cannot share screens or hear each other.

4. *Blocker:* User data is corrupted or leaked. Nothing breaks trust as much as the loss of users' data. At Miro, we had a mantra, "User data is sacred." Eventually, it will happen to any product that has users, so have regularly updated backups.

Like any other model, this tier segregation is a vast simplification that should be seen as a gradient, and it heavily depends on business circumstances. If you make a graphic design tool, probably you should rate rendering defects higher than if you're working on an accounting system. If you make a payment provider, you should pay more attention to number precision than if you're creating a video game.

What Is a Critical Flow?

Think of the main reason your product exists and the key action leading to it. For Framer, it's publishing a site. For Booking.com, it's reserving a hotel. For Google Drive, it's uploading a file. People can deal with missing information, a broken layout, and a lagging UI where they need to refresh a page to get the desired result, but if they cannot publish a site or book a hotel, everything else in the product is meaningless, however good it is. This key sequence of user actions leading to the goal is called *critical flow*.

Estimating Bug Reach

By picking high-severity bugs, we choose the worst of the issues and are thus striving for the greatest happiness for the greatest number of users. To select issues concerning the most people, or, in other words, optimize for the greatest number, we'll use a powerful technique known as guesstimation.

Use the force of approximation, which is also known as an educated guess. In their book *Guesstimation*,[1] full of fun and colorful examples, Lawrence Weinstein and John Adam lay out a beautiful way of approximating. The gist of it is this:

- Break down the value into compounds.
- Round all the compounds you can't know exactly to the nearest factor of ten (0.01, 0.1, 1, 10, 100, and so on). It's easy to do in your head and often is good enough.
- If a compound value can vary broadly (order of magnitude or more), estimate lower and upper boundaries for each of them (factors of ten will do) and take the geometric mean of them. For example, the geometric mean of 5 and 20 is 10, because $10 = \sqrt{5 \times 20}$. Feel free to factor it and round to the closest value you can approximate the square root of.
- Check plausibility: compare the answer to a known value of a similar metric. If it's an order of magnitude different from what you expected, restart and dig deeper: break down into more detailed compounds, and round with higher precision where you can.

"Dare to be imprecise," as Weinstein and Adam put it in their book.

Guesstimation Exercise

How many electric bicycles are there in Amsterdam? It's hard to tell straight away. A thousand? A million? Let's approximate. How many people are living in Amsterdam, rounded to the factor of 10? 100,000 is probably too few; 10 million is way too many. 1,000,000 will do. How many bicycles are there per person? 0.1 is too few, 10 is too many. Let it be 1. What percentage of bicycles are electric? Hard to say without observation, but we can set boundaries. Surely, more than 1 in 100, but less than half. So, we'll use the geometric mean of the two:

$$\sqrt{0.5 \times 0.01} = \sqrt{0.005} = \sqrt{0.05 \times 0.1} \approx \sqrt{0.04} \times \sqrt{0.09} = 0.2 \times 0.3 = 0.06$$

So, let it be 6 in 100. The real result would be $\sqrt{0.005} \approx 0.07071$. Not too far off! We can say that in Amsterdam, there are approximately $1\,000\,000 \times 1 \times 0.06 = 60\,000$ e-bikes.

Our approximation is 60,000 e-bikes, which does not seem implausible for Amsterdam. The real value was 57,000 in 2021.[a] Surprisingly close, isn't it?

a. https://onderzoek.amsterdam.nl/artikel/verkeer-in-cijfers-2024#hoeveel-gebruik-maken-amsterdammers-van-andere-manieren-van-vervoer

1. https://press.princeton.edu/books/paperback/9780691129495/guesstimation

Estimating Bug Fix Time

Estimation of development time is notoriously hard, especially when it comes to bugs. The very nature of a bug is the combination of known unknowns and unknown unknowns.

The developer community even saw the rise and fall of a movement called #noestimates. They advocate against estimating engineering tasks in principle. They say that accurate estimation is impossible, and inaccurate estimates will only put unnecessary pressure on the team, so estimation as such is waste. According to #noestimates[2] proponents, there are only two valid estimations for a given task: 1 if it fits a sprint, and ∞ if it doesn't. They have a point, and we might witness the rise of the movement again in the future, but as of 2025, #noestimate is followed by a marginal minority of teams. You'll have to estimate.

On top of known unknowns and unknown unknowns, I want to introduce a concept of known unknown unknowns—and I claim you can use that. Let's put things straight with the known unknowns first. Often you're aware in advance of some important missing pieces of information you need in order to fix the issue. Those are your known unknowns, and you often can quickly estimate them. Along the way, you'll probably hit one or two unknown unknowns—missing pieces of information to cover important knowledge gaps you didn't foresee. However, when you're familiar with the context, you can estimate the number and size of the gaps usually occurring in similar situations, turning them into known unknown unknowns, and you can reasonably forecast how much time it might take. Sometimes you know what you don't know; sometimes you don't know what you don't know; and sometimes you know what you don't know that you don't know, and you can use that knowledge.

My take: "I feel like the bug will take this long" is a perfectly valid estimate justification, given that you know the codebase well and have no vivid tendency of over- or underestimating tasks. Your first, fast, automatic, and intuitive response is suggested by System 1, a cognitive mode constantly processing piles of information in your brain without you even trying to deliberately analyze any of it. I know, your PMs will ask for a better justification they can pass on to the leadership, but I'm sure you can come up with something. The following are several methodologies you can use to quickly and reasonably estimate bug fixes. At least, you'll be able to give plausible justifications to made up guesstimates while looking smart.

---

2. https://engineering.zalando.com/posts/2018/11/no-estimates.html

Estimation by Analogy

"The bug is in core engine; they take three days to fix on average" or "The component state is not being updated; should take 30 minutes"—both sound convincing. At first glance, they're close to "I feel like it's this long," but there's an important difference. Asked "Why?" you can respond with historical data.

Be prepared. Basic preparations will take you an hour and save you days of back-and-forth.

1. Choose an estimation unit. Hours, days, or story points.
2. Break the continuum of estimates into a finite set of values. Fibonacci numbers are the gold standard in Agile, but I've seen people using powers of 2 and T-shirt sizes (XS to XXL).
3. Create a list of reference bugs for each possible estimation option. Ideally, they should all be real historical examples in the same product from not too long ago.
4. When asked "How long will the bug take?," compare the bug with each list item and find the most similar one in terms of complexity.

You'll enjoy more uninterrupted time, and your manager will be proud of you.

Three-Point Estimation

The big problem of estimating with many unknowns, common in bugs, is that you don't know how big the task is until it's done. But if you're familiar with the codebase and have experience of similar work, you know how many moving parts the system has and can figure out how badly things potentially can go. In other words, you project worst-case and best-case scenarios, as well as estimate the most likely of them, and deduct a single number from them.

Estimate three values for the bug fix:

- *Optimistic (O):* The best-case scenario where the fix is straightforward.
- *Pessimistic (P):* The worst-case scenario where the bug is more complex than initially thought.
- *Most Likely (M):* The most probable scenario based on the team's experience.

Calculate the final estimate using the formula called Program Evaluation and Review Technique, or PERT:

$$\frac{O + 4 \times M + P}{6}$$

Or, speaking our other common language, we have this:

```
const threePointEstimation = (
    optimistic: number,
    pessimistic: number,
    mostLikely: number
) => (
    optimistic +
    4 * mostLikely +
    pessimistic
) / 6
```

Timeboxing

You can address the "How long is it going to take?" question in several ways now. However, often it's not the right question to ask. Sometimes, the better question is "How much time are we ready to spend on it?"—meaning that if the task takes too long to solve, it's better to not solve it at all and do something else instead.

In most situations, when the task is not critical, you want to timebox it, but base your timebox on a reasonable time estimate and expected value. Timeboxing allows for better time management, preventing a minor problem from eating up all the time. Constraints drive creativity. A strict time limit encourages teams to find efficient, creative solutions. Also, timeboxing saves time spent on estimation. Rather than spending time trying to reach consensus on whether the task is big or small, you agree on how long would be appropriate to spend, and move on. Less useless talking, more productive work, everyone wins.

When you leave a task unfinished, it can feel like the time spent on it has been wasted. It's not—if you leave notes that will make it easy to pick up the investigation from where you stopped, not begin from scratch. We'll talk more about writing a lab notebook in Chapter 4, Finding the Root Cause, on page 39.

You can combine timeboxing with classic methods of estimation: for example, if a bug has more than one solution, one fast and one clean, you can timebox the clean, and if you can't implement it in reasonable time, go for the easy one. If a bug consists of many subparts and some of them are optional, timebox the optional. If you want to do the refactoring as a preparation for a bug fix, definitely timebox it, because, like a painting, refactoring is never done, only abandoned.

Prioritizing Bugs Using RICE

Priority is a function of reach, severity, and time. You want to tackle first the worst of the issues, concerning the most people, that is the fastest to solve, and now, when you're able to evaluate all three parameters, you want to combine them into a single metric, but how do you do it? Do you take first a small issue concerning a lot of people or a severe one concerning only one? What if one of the issues is easier to resolve? The three metrics are measured in different units, and combining them is not straightforward.

Let's assume that you have two known bugs in an application with 1,000 daily users.

1. Two users reported that they cannot register in your application because their full names are 52 characters long, and you have a validation limit set to 50.
2. All users of your application experience slow initial loading. They see a loading indicator for around five seconds.

First, kudos for having a thousand users and only two known bugs. Awesome result! Usually it's the other way around. You need to choose one to take first. This might seem like a trivial exercise, but when you have a hundred bugs for a team of five, and you need to balance that with working on new features, you better have a good methodology at hand.

One common way of prioritizing bugs is using the RICE score. It stands for Reach, Impact, Confidence, Effort, and lets you calculate a single numeric value for every task to sort your bug backlog by.

$$\frac{Reach \times Impact \times Confidence}{Effort}$$

Be aware that such formulas are canonical examples of what the Nobel laureate Paul Romer called "mathiness."[3] Carl T. Bergstrom and Jevin D. West gave many good examples of this in their book *Calling Bullshit*. These expressions "create the impression of rigor and accuracy," which we expect of anything that looks mathematical, but on a closer look we find out that it involves a good share of guesswork, operations on barely related units, and an arbitrarily chosen multiplicator, so don't try treating the RICE score the same way as measurements.

Nevertheless, use them without a doubt in situations where reaching an agreement and moving on is preferable to finding the best possible solution

3. https://paulromer.net/mathiness/

at the cost of time spent on discussions. These situations are very common in product development. All models are wrong, but some are useful. If you get a score of 100 on one item and 5 on another, you can confidently prioritize the former over the latter.

Reach

Estimate the absolute number of users who encounter this bug. If the bug is reproduced only in Safari, you can prorate this number by the share of Safari users (around 15%–20% overall as I'm writing this, and can vary depending on your audience profile). If the bug is in a part of the site that you know only a quarter of users bother visiting, divide it by 4. If it's only for users using a particular locale, divide accordingly.

Keep in mind that often people don't report bugs. Use your best judgment to approximate how many people can be possibly affected. How many users of your app do you think have full names over 50 characters long?

For our case, we assume it's 2 people for bug #1 and 1,000 for bug #2.

Impact

You can rate severity, or how bad the bug is, on a scale from 0.25 to 4.

In our example, not being able to log in is just about as bad as it can be. Only a serious data loss would be worse. It would be fair to rate it at 2 or even 4. By contrast, waiting for five seconds to load is noticeable but causes at worst a minor disturbance. 0.25 or 0.5 would be a good impact estimate, depending on your performance requirements.

Confidence

Confidence is the rating of how sure you are that the approximations of effort and reach are correct. Don't calculate too hard, and choose between 100 if you're fully confident, 80 if you're aware of some unknowns, or 50 if there are significant unknowns. If you believe 50 is too much, you shouldn't be picking this until you resolve some of the most significant unknowns.

Effort

RICE can be seen as a cost-benefit analysis, where reach, impact, and confidence combined measure the benefits of resolving the bug, and effort is the single score representing the costs, or how much developer time you think it will take to fix the problem. The original RICE model developed in Intercom used developer-month as a unit of effort with anything less than a month rated as 0.5, but if you find yourself in a faster-paced project and lucky to have some granularity of tasks, using month as a unit doesn't make much sense, and trying to estimate a project large enough to fill several months will likely fail without proper decomposition anyway. In practice, it's easier to not introduce new entities into the process, and use whatever measure you already have in use, be it weeks, days, hours, or story points.

If the supposed fix is a matter of changing a constant in the validation schema, and you have an idea where this constant is, you can get the minimal possible estimate: five minutes in a day, depending on the company processes. If it's a matter of changing database schema to support longer values, that's a whole other story. In our example, we assume that it's a constant.

Prioritizing Beyond Methodologies

Whatever you do, don't be a dogmatic follower. Be smart, use reason. You'll inevitably break some of the time limits when finishing the task is right thing to do; you'll end up using some combination of estimation, no estimation, and timeboxing, depending on circumstances.

Business needs will impact your priorities too, and you'll have to evaluate that on a case-by-case basis. Imagine that the company logo is missing in the application. Users might not care at all if they can use the app and solve their needs, but the business you own or work for needs branding to be visible, so you'll have to take that into account.

Techniques and methodologies are tools, and you're free to use or not use them to get things done.

Wrapping Up

Now that you've completed this chapter, you should be able to determine severity and reach of a bug using approximations, and time to fix it using three-point estimation. You should be able to compare relative priority of bugs against one another using RICE.

In the next chapter, we'll talk about the organization of the bug fixing process: how to reproduce, investigate, and analyze bugs.

CHAPTER 4

Finding the Root Cause

Generally speaking, debugging is a subset of forensics: something bad has happened, and we're trying to prevent it from happening again. More precisely, debugging is a form of forensic engineering to the same extent that software engineering is a form of engineering. The methods mechanical or electric engineers use to troubleshoot their systems are often applicable to software debugging, and the lingo we use in the debugging discourse is largely borrowed from there.

Just like troubleshooting a complex mechanism, solving an issue in a complex software system requires understanding its cause.

In this chapter, we'll cover how to do the research required to properly fix a bug, which is the largest and the most important part of the whole debugging process. Specifically, you'll learn to use root-cause analysis and a failure analysis tree to find a point where the fix will be the most effective. You'll learn to use the scientific method and share your findings to make sure the problems you fix never reappear.

To follow along with this chapter, you won't need any special technical knowledge.

Finding the Reproduction Steps

You can't fix what you can't see. Worse, until you know the exact steps to consistently, predictably achieve the problematic state you intend to fix, you don't know whether you need to fix it. Even the worst-sounding bug report turns out unimportant if it happens, say, only on a specific old version of a certain browser. An easy solution is to kindly ask the user to update the browser, which happens automatically nowadays anyway.

Exact reproduction steps make sure you fix the right thing. If a report mentions "lost recent user input," you might instinctively start looking for mistakes in data layers, but if you ask more questions and figure out that the user had a bad internet connection and the data had never been transferred to the server at all, you'll consider different sorts of solutions: you might want to clearly inform the user that the connection is broken, preserve the data locally to be sent after the connection is restored, or implement a retry mechanism. The point is that solutions you find for a problem you don't understand well will not be optimal.

Now, if we agree that reproduction steps are essential, let's talk about how to systematically find them.

Start with a Good Bug Report Template

You'll need a bug report template, which users will use to send you bug reports. It must be small, all its fields should be optional, and it must be crystal clear that they are optional. Let the user copy all the relevant debug information at once. Reporting a bug is an act of goodwill, so make it as easy as possible. What can be automated should be automated. The goal of the template is not to filter out low-quality reports but to politely hint to the user what you need to know to help.

You should put questions on the template that you keep asking over and over again, like these for example:

- What did you do before experiencing the issue?
- What exactly happened?
- What should have happened?
- When did it happen?
- How often does it happen?
- Did you see any error messages?
- What is your:
  - Operating system?
  - Browser?
  - Hardware specs?
  - Screen size?
- Can you provide a screenshot?

Don't force the user to fill in all the info, and be sure to leave space for free-form notes. Some of these questions will be irrelevant for most of the bugs, so please, again, don't force users to fill everything in. And, most importantly, do not close the ticket with a "Works for me" response. People do not forgive that.

Reproduction Steps

The trio of Action-Expectation-Reality is the very minimal definition of a bug. If any of these components are missing, you waste time—either failing to reproduce the issue or trying to catch a bug that doesn't exist.

Usually, the trio takes this form:

1. *Action:* Steps to reproduce the issue.
2. *Expectation:* The desired result after the action.
3. *Reality:* The actual result you get instead of the desired one.

Screenshots and videos help tremendously, as do error messages and logs.

Steps to reproduce should be specific enough to follow. They should describe the initial state, then list discrete, consequential steps, preferably also describing the result of the state after each step. Description should be minimal and not include any misleading details.

Writing a good bug description is a hard job, even after you've done it many times. Don't offload this burden on users, especially if they're not software developers. Politely ask them to describe steps along with expected and actual results, but do not expect the description to be concise and comprehensive. You'll have to refine it on your own.

You'll learn to match patterns in bug descriptions with certain types of problems. For example, if you see that something happens "occasionally" or "sometimes," you probably should be looking for race conditions in asynchronous operations like network requests or workers. If you see that a page "freezes" or "crashes," you should start profiling memory or CPU. If you see that something has long delays, you probably should optimistically update the local state or show a loading indicator, depending on your UX design preferences. If you see a `NaN` value, you should start looking for division by zero or non-numeric types in numeric operations.

A good bug report saves time. Tell the users what would make it good for you and make it easy to get this data. Help them by enriching the bug report with technical info automatically.

Reproducing Browser-Specific Bugs

You have a bug reported only in a specific browser—let's say, Safari. But the problem is you have only a Windows machine. Or you have Linux, but you need to investigate a bug in Internet Explorer (I sincerely hope not) or in an older version of Chrome. How do you reproduce it? How do you verify that this bug is indeed browser-specific?

You can run a virtual machine (VM) with the browser of choice locally using Docker or VM software like Microsoft Hyper-V, VirtualBox, or VMWare. Easier, but paid, is to run a browser version in the cloud and test it right on the web using the likes of BrowserStack, DataDog, and LambdaTest.

Last piece of advice: if you confirm that users experience the bug only in an old version of a browser, just ask them to update or wait a bit until it happens automatically. Don't waste your time fixing a problem that will go away by itself.

Automate the Data Collection

Useful technical details such as browser version, operating system, and error text are very annoying to collect manually but can be trivially collected using standard Web APIs. When it comes to computers, "the hard problems are easy, and the easy problems are hard," as Steven Pinker puts it in *Language Instinct [Pin07]*. Be nice to the users and solve for them the hard problem that is easy. For instance, use the global `navigator` property to get browser specs:

```
function getBrowserInfo() {
    return {
        userAgent: navigator.userAgent,
        language: navigator.language,
        cookies: navigator.cookieEnabled,
        localStorage: !!window.localStorage,
    }
}
```

The `navigator` property also contains info about the OS and hardware, such as connection type and number of CPU cores. We'll also add memory usage info.

```
async function getSystemInfo() {
    const usedMemoryBytes =
        (await performance.measureUserAgentSpecificMemory()).bytes
    return {
        platform: navigator.platform,
        cores: navigator.hardwareConcurrency,
        memory: `${usedMemoryBytes  / (1024 * 1024)} MB`,
        connection: navigator.connection?.effectiveType,
    }
}
```

measureUserAgentSpecificMemory is the recommended way of measuring memory since performance.memory got deprecated and excluded from web standards.

measureUserAgentSpecificMemory may be not available

At publication time, measureUserAgentSpecificMemory is experimental and Chromium-only. If it isn't available in your browser, use the deprecated performance.memory function.

Next, let's collect screen information:

```
function getScreenInfo()  {
    return {
        width: screen.width,
        height: screen.height,
        colorDepth: screen.colorDepth,
        pixelRatio: window.devicePixelRatio,
        orientation: screen.orientation.type,
    }
}
```

It'll be handy to know what version of the application was used to identify, for example, cache invalidation problems or to find out on which exact page of your website the bug was found.

```
function getAppInfo()  {
    return {
        /*
            Here goes your release version or build number,
             usually generated during compile time
        */
        version: '1.0.0',
        url: window.location.href,
        viewport: {
            width: window.innerWidth,
            height: window.innerHeight,
        },
        timestamp: new Date().toISOString(),
    }
}
```

Note that some of these properties will not be available in WebWorkers, worklets, and Node.js, where there's no window property available.

On top of that, these same properties are widely used by advertising companies for fingerprinting and can be used by evil actors for all sorts of online surveillance. Most ad-blocking software and privacy-focused browsers will skew or hinder some data.

With that in mind, let's combine all the data in a single object that we'll ask the user to include in the error report:

```
function collectEnvironmentInfo() {
  return {
    browser: getBrowserInfo(),
    screen: getScreenInfo(),
    system: getSystemInfo(),
    app: getAppInfo()
  }
}
```

If you have an error boundary, as we discussed in Chapter 1, Printing and Interpreting Errors, on page 1, you can and probably should attach this information to the error report and even send it automatically. Remember to respect user privacy. Do not include any personal information and do not store the reports any longer than you need. It's unethical and even illegal in many countries, notably in the European Union.

Specialized monitoring software like Sentry and Logdy includes environment information in its error reports, so if you use it in your application, you won't have to manually collect this data. We'll talk more about observability in Chapter 5, Designing Software That Doesn't Break, on page 53.

Using Systems of Root-Cause Analysis

You can fix most bugs in more than one possible way, and the most obvious way is almost always not the best. Imagine a login screen where authentication fails with a timeout. An obvious solution would be to increase the timeout. Go for it if you urgently need an immediate solution, but don't stop there. What caused a 3-second timeout today might start causing a 10-second timeout tomorrow.

In other words, before asking yourself How do I solve it?, ask Why does it happen?, then ask it again, and again.

The Five Why's

The simplest root-cause analysis technique is the iterative self-interrogation commonly known as the Five Why's. You ask why, and on every answer you ask "Why is that?" until you reach the root cause. Five is just an arbitrary number.

The problem: the browser freezes when interacting with the data table. Let's ask, "Why?"

1. Why? Extreme usage of CPU and memory when sorting or filtering the table.
2. Why? The application is re-rendering the entire table (all 1,000+ rows) for every user interaction, even minor ones.
3. Why? The table is using a naive implementation that doesn't implement virtual scrolling or incremental updates.
4. Why? The development team built a custom table component instead of using an established library because of specific design requirements.
5. Why? The component was initially tested with small datasets (20–30 rows) during development, but in production, users regularly work with datasets of 1,000+ rows, revealing the performance limitations.

As a result, you find a good fix that addresses problems discovered on all levels:

1. Implement virtual scrolling to render only visible rows.
2. Support incremental updates to modify only changed cells.
3. Implement pagination as a fallback for large datasets.
4. Negotiate to change design requirements in a way that we can use a good library for the table.
5. Add performance benchmarks to the CI/CD pipeline with realistic data volumes.

You'll notice that with every iteration of Why? you make, your answers will drift in a certain direction. Sometimes they become more and more technical (we do not remove references to old state to release memory) and sometimes more and more organizational (our process does not include a QA verification step). The direction of the drift is a good hint to where you can make the most impact—on the technical side or on the organizational side.

Never use people as the root cause. Never. The reason is simple: it doesn't help. People are hard to change, and they're out of your control. They're easy to replace only in theory, if you have the mandate. But in practice, both a technical solution and a process improvement will be easier, faster, and more efficient than finding more suitable people or trying to change the humans.

The human factor does matter, though. To the same question Why is the whole table re-rendering on any minor change?, a QA engineer will reply "because we didn't have performance tests to catch the bug during testing." A front-end engineer will tell you that "we haven't implemented smart change detection," and a product manager will tell you that "we hadn't defined clear nonfunctional requirements." All three are correct and will lead to different solutions. This difference naturally leads me to the next technique, called Failure Tree, which is a nonlinear version of the Five Why's.

Using the Failure Tree

The failure tree is a technique widely used in aerospace, nuclear, and chemical industries to prevent and investigate malfunctions. To identify the root cause of an issue by using a failure tree, start with a concise description of the bug: "Browser freezes," or "Login button does not respond," or "Page scroll jumps to the top." This is the stem of your tree, or the root, if you prefer.

Then broadly define domains that potentially could cause it.

- Rendering problems.
- JavaScript issues.
- Data volume issues.

Write them down as tree branches. Then you get more specific: What kind of JavaScript issue could have caused the bug?

- Event handler problem.
- Memory management.
- Inefficient data processing.

Branch them out from "JavaScript issues" and do the same for their siblings. Then get even more specific: What kind of event handler problem?

- Expensive calculations in handler methods.
- Event handler throttling missing.
- Event delegation isn't implemented.

Failure trees barely ever need more than three nesting levels.

Any mind mapping software is a good tool to draw such a tree (as shown in the image). Analyze and test each branch from leaves to the stem, starting with the ones that are the easiest to verify.

The beauty of the failure tree is that you can use it preventively, as do engineers in heavy industries. First-level branches are large components of the system and what can possibly go wrong with each one of them. Similarly, QA engineers create test plans and design test cases.

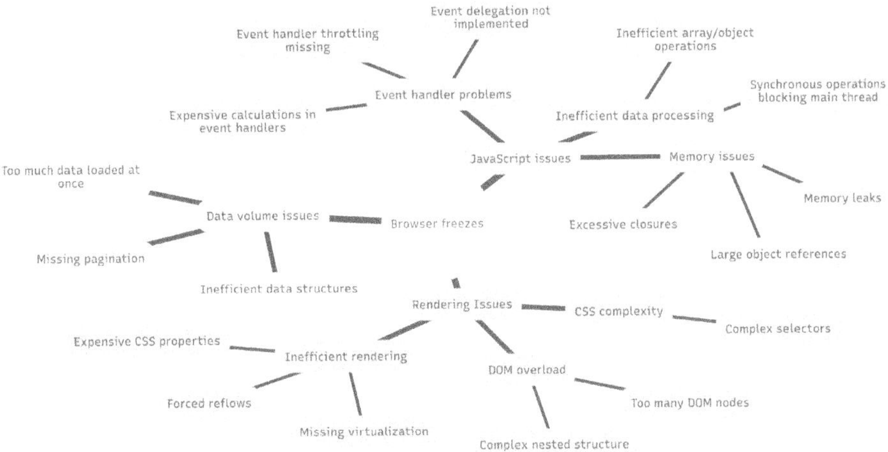

Using the Scientific Method

Computers are dumb, which is beautiful. They are finite automata predictably transforming input bits into output bits, and everything an automaton outputs has a perfectly reasonable explanation bounded within the input bits or the automaton itself. Sometimes output bytes don't match our expectations, so we start studying the system to find the parts responsible for the mismatch, and we call them bugs. Once a plausible explanation is found, it can be verified. The deterministic nature of computers allows that. This enables us to iteratively refine and test hypotheses because running an experiment is instantaneous and cheap.

Debugging has many parallels with the scientific method, and we can learn many practical lessons from scientists. Let's treat a debugging session as a study and put the science back into computer science. The scientific method is a time-tested framework for making discoveries, and a discovery is exactly what we need so we can fix a bug. Descriptions of the scientific method vary, but they always include a variation of the same loop:

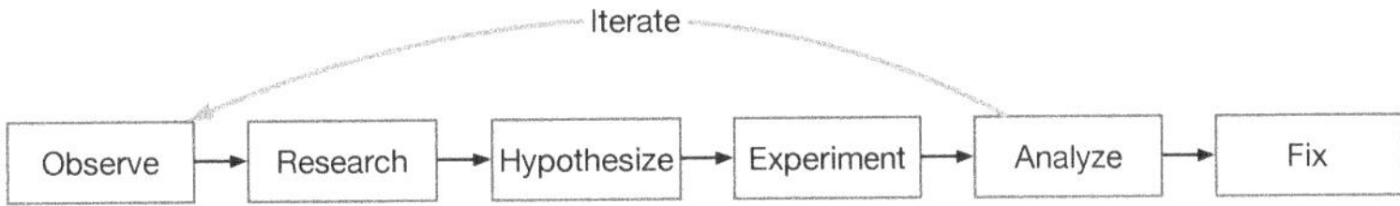

In the following sections, we'll apply the steps of the scientific method—Observe, Research, Hypothesize, Experiment, Analyze, Iterate—to the debugging process while keeping notes in a lab notebook.

Observe

Look. Don't guess why, don't try to fix, don't intervene, don't build conclusions—it all will only obstruct the view at this stage. If your notes are short, chaotic, and silly, that's good. Don't waste your time creating fancy hierarchies and templates. Short notes are easier to navigate.

Write down in your lab notebook:

- Steps you take.
- Results you get.
- Logs and error messages.

Research

Look up the error message. Yes, you can search StackOverflow or ask a Large Language Model (LLM), but the first thing I usually do is search Slack and Notion, where all our internal communications are. Solutions within the context of your product tend to be more relevant.

When googling and looking up the error message in internal channels doesn't help, explaining the problem to someone is the next logical step. Rubber ducks are mostly being replaced by explaining a problem to LLMs. From my experience, it still works better if your counterpart is a human being. Then you're forced to phrase the problem description in such a way that a person whose context awareness and thinking patterns are similar to yours would understand. Write down relevant findings into the lab notebook.

Hypothesize

Come up with a plausible explanation for the bug. Any hypothesis that doesn't contradict itself or the observations is good.

When you have several equally plausible hypotheses, Occam's razor is a good heuristic to choose one. "Entities should not be multiplied needlessly" means that you should prefer the simplest of the competing theories. Of course, it doesn't always mean it's going to be the right one.

Experiment

Check if your hypothesis is true. Use minimally invasive probes. Log, assert, and use an interactive debugger. Don't significantly alter the system and don't attempt to fix the bug yet. Try to predict other oddities that should occur if your hypothesis is correct and check if they indeed occur.

Predictability and the deterministic nature of computers make experiments almost free and very reliable. Take advantage of it.

Analyze

If the hypothesis was wrong, refine it or propose a new one. In other words, iterate. Ask yourself:

- What changed?
- Was the problem fixed?
  - If yes, what caused the problem?
  - If no, what are your findings?

The findings can be these, for example:

- New error messages.
- Behavior change.

Keep a Lab Notebook

An essential part of any research is a lab notebook. Why keep it? Two reasons: cognitive load and knowledge sharing.

While debugging a complex issue, you have to keep many things in your head. Sometimes too many. Cognitive load is what we call the number of things you have to process simultaneously. Writing things down offloads them from your internal RAM to disk, so your brain can run fewer background tasks and focus on what matters at the moment. Make sure your writing makes some sense so that you can load the information back to RAM from the disk later. I promise I won't stretch the metaphor any further.

Cognitive load reduction makes your current debugging session easier, but knowledge-sharing simplifies the next one when someone else encounters a similar bug. Make sure your notes are stored in a place where people will be able to find them. One of those people might be you.

Reduce Intellectual Debt

"I don't know why it works, but it works" can be a good short-term solution. But if you don't know why something works, you don't know if it breaks something else or if it will work just as well under different circumstances. If you repeatedly rely on decisions made without proper understanding, they quickly snowball into a big pile of fragile legacy code that everyone is afraid to touch because it unpredictably breaks, and the product development effectively stops. That being said, "Try random stuff and see if it breaks" is a good approach for exploratory testing or to unblock yourself when you're stuck. It mustn't be the last step in this process, because it increases intellectual debt.

Intellectual debt is the term coined by Jonathan Zittrain in 2018. His text "The Hidden Costs of Automated Thinking"[1] aged too well to believe it was written in the pre-LLM era:

> This approach to discovery—answers first, explanations later—accrues what I call intellectual debt. It's possible to discover what works without knowing why it works, and then to put that insight to use immediately, assuming that the underlying mechanism will be figured out later. In some cases, we pay off this intellectual debt quickly. But in others, we let it compound, relying, for decades, on knowledge that's not fully known.

By analogy, technical debt is where we trade off internal quality in favor of product value or delivery speed, while intellectual debt is the lack of understanding we accept in exchange for the empirically achieved result. We call these debt for a reason: eventually, you'll have to pay it back. Interest rates apply.

Leave Artifacts

The fix is, of course, the most important goal of any debugging session, but there are many other artifacts you can leave that will help you long-term—the lab notebook is only one of them.

Here are others, ordered from easy to hard:

1. Leave a code comment.
2. Add a unit test.
3. Update documentation.
4. Write a post or give a talk.

Not every bugfix deserves a documentation update, and even less deserve a post or talk, but a code comment or a unit test serves two purposes. First, they make it explicit that the change is intentional. It's especially important when your fix seems bizarre or hacky. Second, they serve as a safeguard against someone else accidentally breaking it again in the future. One important notion is that a unit test is better than a comment. Another is that a good comment shouldn't describe what the code does, but rather why. The "what" should be clear from the code itself.

---

1. https://www.newyorker.com/tech/annals-of-technology/the-hidden-costs-of-automated-thinking

Just as blackbirds or marmots alarm their peers of danger by a distinct squeaky sound, you save your peers from trouble by sharing your mistakes and how you mitigated them. Leaving a trace of artifacts raises learning from mistakes from the personal to interpersonal level. Not only are you less likely to fall into the same traps but also, thanks to the shared knowledge, so are your peers.

Finding the Suspect Commit Using git bisect

Once you've found good reproduction steps and can easily verify if a version is working or not, you unlock a quick way to find the fix empirically rather than analytically.

For new bugs where existing correct behavior was broken, and you know a point in time when it was working, one of the quickest ways is `git bisect`—assuming that you're using Git and your commit history is at least somewhat meaningful.

Find a known good commit in history where you're sure the bug did not exist. Save its hash. For example, to find a commit by its message, run this:

```
git log --oneline | grep -i "working change"
```

Identify the current bad commit—this is usually the latest commit:

```
git log --oneline -1
```

Start bisecting:

```
git bisect start
git bisect bad <bad-commit-hash>
git bisect good <good-commit-hash>
```

Git will check out a midpoint commit. Now, manually test your front end.

If your project is using `vite` or `webpack` and the commit wasn't too far in the past, you might even get the application hot-reloaded. Otherwise, build the project:

```
yarn build
```

And run the dev server:

```
yarn dev
```

Open the application in the browser and check the UI for the bug.

Mark the current commit good or bad:

```
git bisect bad # if bad
get bisect good # if good
```

Repeat steps until Git narrows it down to the exact commit that introduced the bug:

```
git bisect reset
```

Inspect the culprit:

```
git show <commit-hash>
```

If you like algorithms, you might have noticed that `git bisect` is a binary search, which means that you can find the causing change among 30 commits in at most 5 steps, and among 1,000 commits in at most 10 steps.

Wrapping Up

Software engineering by its nature stands somewhere in-between heavy industries and science, so we eagerly adopt the techniques from both. In this chapter, we combined them with authentic programming practices, transforming them into solutions to the problems we face.

After reading this chapter, you should be able to write effective bug reports. To make bug reports more helpful, you're now able to automatically collect technical details using Web APIs. You now can find the root cause of the problem using Five Why's and failure tree analysis and use the scientific method researching the bug. Finally, to make sure the things you fix don't break again, you know what artifacts to leave after the problem is resolved.

These techniques require consistent practice to become habits, and you'll have to put in deliberate effort at the beginning to start practicing them—double so if you already have an established process you intend to change. Building and breaking habits is hard. Still, if your process has a problem that can be fixed with one of these practices, implementing it is an easy and effective solution with long-lasting results.

CHAPTER 5

Designing Software That Doesn't Break

The best bug is the one that never was. Just like disease and crime prevention programs are an order of magnitude more effective than mitigation, bug prevention is one of the best time investments in software development. Catch bugs before releasing them, and you won't have to look for them all over the place.

Conversely, the absolute worst scenario is when a bug is continuously causing harm without being detected or reported. Having angry people asking today, "Why is your app not working?" is preferable to the same people asking more angrily tomorrow, "What happened to my data?"

A Bug Becomes a Feature

When a known bug lives long enough and becomes part of the usual landscape, you cannot fix it anymore without breaking backward compatibility. This is exactly what happened to early JavaScript, leading to the infamous result of `typeof null`.

`typeof null === 'object'` has been true since JavaScript was born in 1995. In its original implementation, values were represented in memory using a type tag and a value. The type tag for objects was `0`, and `null` was represented as the NULL pointer (which was essentially all zeros in memory). Since the type tag portion of null was 0, it was incorrectly identified as an object when the `typeof` operator was applied.

Despite being recognized as a bug, this behavior has never been corrected because changing it would potentially break existing code, and JavaScript has been aiming to be fully backward compatible through the years. A proposal to fix this in ECMAScript 6 was rejected.

The image of bug-free software is pure, utopian fantasy. However, the middle ground between "no bug was ever released" and "multiple bugs have been causing harm while staying unnoticed" is wide enough to place many safety nets. They increase your chances for intercepting problems while fixing them is still easy and relaxed.

If you draw a flowchart of a software delivery pipeline, you'll probably get something like this, give or take:

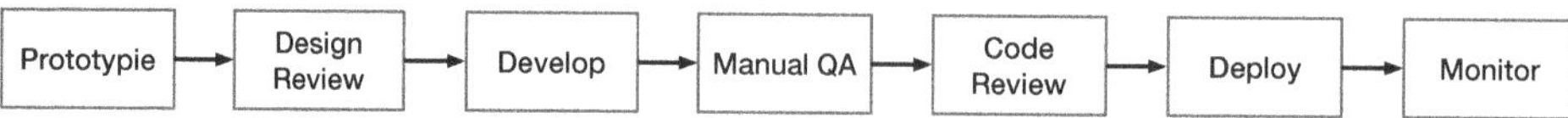

The further right your bug reaches, the more heavily it will impact your delivery pipeline, so you want to discover bugs as early as possible, shifting problem discovery to the left. This idea is commonly called shift-left testing, and it usually involves adding some form of testing or quality practice to every stage of the pipeline.

For example, clean code and appropriate usage of patterns will help you avoid bugs caused by misunderstanding. Static analysis and unit tests prevent human mistakes and check known corner cases at a low level. Integration tests and smoke tests make sure the units work together well as a system. Dogfooding and beta testing let the real users notice issues before they reach a wider audience. Monitoring and alerting let you notice problems before they get reported or even noticed by users, and logging lets you find the root cause faster. Fast deployment lets you easily revert the product to a stable version once an incident happens.

In this chapter, we'll learn to set up every stage of the feature delivery pipeline to detect a portion of problems, step by step, starting with clean code.

Write Clean Code

Clean code breaks less; it's a fact. Not because it works any better—it's not usually the case. The real reason is that clean code is easier to read and understand, so changing it leads to more predictable results.

Clean code is written with maintainability in mind, with regard to the reader. Its author's intentions are clear, and style is consistent. It's hard to precisely define, but you know when you see it. Many classic books, namely *Clean Code* by Robert Martin and *Refactoring* by Martin Fowler, explain it in more detail and better than I would ever be able to. Instead of listing techniques and practices, I want to give you one fundamental principle that matters the most when it comes to writing bug-free code. Minimize the cognitive load.

You will always find multiple ways of doing one thing. Some ways are clever, some are easy, some are beautiful, some feel good in the process, some work fast, or some are short. My advice is choose the one that requires fewer brain cells to understand. In other words, optimize the cognitive load for the people who will maintain your code.

What is clean code? Code you can understand and maintain with a minimal cognitive load. Why should you aim to write clean code? Because it reduces cognitive load and lets people maintaining code focus on things that really matter: building a better web, making money, hacking, learning, having fun with code, and so on. Ultimately, cognitive load is what matters.

Prettify Code on Commit

Here are two equivalent functions. Each has a bug. Note how much easier it is to spot the bug in the second one:

```
function sumEvens(numbers:number[]){
let total= 0;
for( const num of numbers ) {
    if(num % 2!==0)
    total += num
}
return total
}

function sumEvens(numbers: number[]): number {
    let total = 0;
    for (const num of numbers) {
        if (num % 2 !== 0) {
            total += num;
        }
    }
    return total;
}
```

Consistent formatting is so easy to enforce technically, and it lets you focus on more important things. Use Prettier to format code, and make sure everyone else is using it too. It's a great tool for helping you maintain your code. Add a pre-commit hook that will prettify all staged files. Run in the root of the repository. Probably, the easiest way to do it is to run one command that does this:

```
npx mrm@2 lint-staged
```

If you want to minimize the number of third-party tools in the project and don't want to install husky, lint-staged, or anything beside Prettier, I feel for you. You can use a more low-level approach and create a .git/hooks/pre-commit file with the following content:

```
#!/bin/sh
# Get names of changed files
FILES=$(git diff --cached --name-only --diff-filter=ACMR | sed 's| |\\ |g')
[ -z "$FILES" ] && exit 0

# Prettify all selected files
echo "$FILES" | xargs ./node_modules/.bin/prettier --ignore-unknown --write

# Add back the modified/prettified files to staging
echo "$FILES" | xargs git add

exit 0
```

Then give the file an execute permission:

```
chmod ug+x .git/hooks/*
```

Now Prettier will uniformly format all files before they're committed by all your team members. It will save your team from some merge conflicts and will free up precious brainpower that would otherwise be busy interpreting spaces and nested brackets.

Rename It, Then Rename It Again

The most important bit of refactoring is naming. Also, it's the hardest one. Just like a good name can make a complex concept clear, a bad name can mislead and cost you hours if not days in the long run. Names must be exactly as long as it takes to be descriptive. Longer is okay, but shorter is not. `isConnected` is a better name than `connectionStatus` for a Boolean because it communicates both contents (Boolean) and meaning (whether the connection is active). However, it becomes a terrible name choice once the variable is expected to have more values than only `true` or `false`—for instance, `pending` or the reason for a disconnection. Precise is better than vague, but vague is still better than misleading.

It's right to change names multiple times during development because the meaning and purpose of the same values change together with the changing context. But once it becomes part of a public interface, each rename becomes a breaking change. Before pushing changes, read the diff and revisit names: make them correct, descriptive, and consistent.

See Values Behind Principles

Ask any developer how to write clean code, and you'll likely be advised to follow a list of principles like the following:

- DRY (don't repeat yourself).
- SOLID (single responsibility, open-closed, Liskov substitution, interface segregation, dependency inversion).

- KISS (keep it simple, stupid).
- YAGNI (you ain't gonna need it).
- "Tell, don't ask."
- "Premature optimization is the root of all evil."

Recommending these principles feels almost like noting that water is wet—too commonsensical to say out loud. But in practice, sometimes it feels wrong to follow these principles, and sometimes you'll find horrifically unmaintainable code that seemingly follows them all. Does it mean that the principles are wrong? Well, maybe. Even if so, they're still useful.

Each principle has a reason to exist, and the reason lies beyond the principle itself. A principle like DRY or KISS is a short, practical advice designed to improve a particular quality of software. There should always be an answer to *why* behind every principle—a value the principle is supposed to protect. This value is more important than the principle.

Do not repeat yourself! Why? Because duplicated code takes double effort to maintain and test. Because it's easy to lose consistency when business logic is duplicated. Because duplicated modules take twice as much disk space (increasing loading time). So what should you do if making a module reusable makes your whole project more complex and fragile (for example, you'd have to move it to a private package and introduce a new step into your pipeline)? What if the extraction of a repeated call into a method makes your whole application work slower (for instance, by adding an extra call stack item in a performance-critical part of the application core)? What if making a generic component adds another level of abstraction and makes the software architecture more complex and less maintainable? In other words, what should you do if following a principle goes against the qualities the principle was designed to support? The answer is straightforward: qualities are more important than principles, so ditch the principle and do repeat yourself!

Learn Design Patterns

Reinventing wheels can be fun and sometimes even justified when a regular wheel doesn't fit your design. But more often than not, this situation reflects your design rather than a wheel. Design patterns are common solutions to common problems. You should learn them not because they're the best solutions possible but because everyone else in the industry learned them too, so being able to fluently speak "singletons" and "decorators" will let you say more with less.

Imagine having to explain that a method you wrote creates an HTMLElement of a different subclass depending on input parameters. You can call it HTMLElementFactory and it will be clear immediately what it does and how to use it.

Don't overuse patterns. Even though reinventing a wheel might lead to a bad design, every wheel must be exactly where it has to be. Remember, boring and predictable code is good. Or, in the words of Brian Kernighan:

> Everyone knows that debugging is twice as hard as writing a program in the first place. So if you're as clever as you can be when you write it, how will you ever debug it?

Let Your Computer Help You

Offload as much routine to machines as you can. It's easy to make sure SyntaxErrors never reach anyone other than the developer writing the code. Code editors, be it Visual Studio Code, WebStorm, or even the web interface of GitHub, easily catch and highlight these errors in milliseconds.

If you're not using a statically typed language like TypeScript or Elm, you should start using one. TypeErrors and ReferenceErrors are simply gone if you use TypeScript and don't work around it.

ESLint is a good addition to Prettier. It highlights problematic code right in your editor and can run on a CI system. It doesn't catch bugs per se, but it points out typical code problems that tend to lead to bugs. Prevention is more effective than mitigation. Shift left, remember?

Don't make a people problem out of a technical problem. If a machine can quickly and reliably do a piece of work, don't make humans do it.

Quality Comes from Culture

Clean code and, by extension, software quality are by-products of culture. The way your team communicates, how they test and review code, how they ship features, and how your team commonly defines shipping in your work environment are all things we call the culture. Culture shapes the decisions made and code created and defines the product quality more than anything else. It's also harder to change than anything else.

Healthy teams build better software, and healthy teams are built of healthy people. Overloaded developers under constant pressure are less likely to have a moment to test an additional corner case or do a casual refactor before merging a change. If people on your team don't feel comfortable asking for help and advice from one another and can't get instant feedback, they're bound to bring bugs that could otherwise be easily avoided. If they tend to ignore code review requests for days or, the other way around, blindly approve everything, they won't ship quality software either.

Culture is hard, but not impossible, to change. To define what a positive change would mean for you in practical terms, do a small exercise: describe the software development culture your team currently has. Address these questions: How often do developers have initiatives? How often do the initiatives get accepted or rejected? How often do you find anything else important about your company culture? Try to stay honest—don't sugarcoat or dramatize the situation. You're the only one who will ever see these answers. Then address the same questions, but this time describe the culture you want to have. In most cases, some items will match, and some will differ from the status quo. Choose up to three most important matching points. These are the ones you want to make an effort to preserve. Choose up to three from the ones that differ. These are the ones you want to change first.

Culture embodies itself in rituals, customs, and communication practices, and company culture is not so different from overall human culture in this regard. Good code review is possible only in an environment where people feel comfortable giving and receiving respectful constructive feedback. People will write unit tests and documentation only when they know their efforts will be appreciated. People will follow the "scout principle" of leaving the code better than they found it only if they trust others to follow it too.

Assure Quality with Automated Testing

We usually describe the desired state of an automated testing suite as "the software testing pyramid," with many unit tests as the foundation, fewer integration tests above it, and even fewer end-to-end (E2E) tests as the tip of the pyramid (illustrated in the following image).

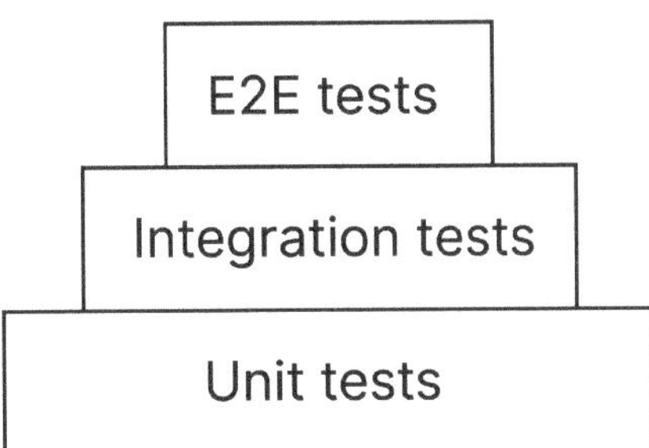

The idea is that having many unit tests is easy because they are so low-maintenance. They're ultra reliable, easy to write, and cheap to run. Ideally, they don't depend on context at all, testing only the module they're supposed to test, and nothing else.

Integration tests are more complex on their own, and the systems they test have more moving parts, sometimes making them a burden to maintain. E2E tests add another level of complexity, requiring headless browsers and snapshotting libraries. They require significant time to run and are flakier.

Of course, the testing pyramid is a desired state for a general case. The real world can differ. For example, during my time at Miro, we had a canvas-based renderer and tightly coupled components, so the only available way of automated testing was screenshot comparisons. They are less deterministic and prone to raising false alarms: every browser version update, and sometimes even a subtle difference in network timings, can create subtle differences in screenshots. But you can employ strategies to avoid false alarms.

First, you can set a threshold in acceptable pixel differences: for example, if less than 2 percent of screenshot pixels differ from the original, the test counts as passed. Second, you can configure the number of retries. Don't set these numbers too high, because higher tolerance negatively affects test reliability, but it's still much better than randomly failing tests you have to restart.

By following the testing pyramid framework, you balance between thorough testing and the efficient use of resources.

I'd like to propose an extension to the testing pyramid framework and add another base layer below the unit tests—assertions (see the following image).

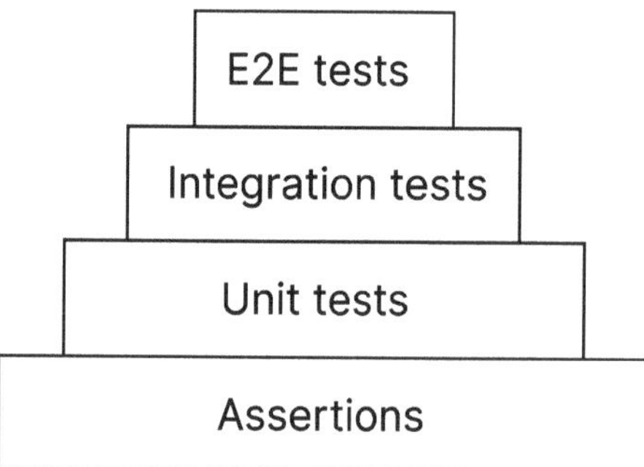

Fail Fast with Runtime Assertions

Shift left means fail fast. Making your program fail faster and louder makes bugs harder to miss, and assertions help to amplify the failures. As a side effect, assertions often will make code cleaner by getting rid of optional chain operators, excessive type checks, and so on.

Let's take as an example a function that takes a string and splits it in single characters:

```
function splitChars(str: string) {
    return str.split('') // returns array of characters
}
```

Looks easy. Now, what if we expect str string, but we're not sure that str is a string? For example, we received it from a server or from user input. We could use an optional chain operator ?.:

```
function splitChars(str: any) {
    return str?.split?.('')
}
```

This is still one line of code. We've added only three characters, but now it's become hard to read, and we had to use any, so it's easy to screw up now. Also, it will break if str happens to have a non-function property called split, and it will return an unexpected result if str is an object with a method split that does something else. Let's improve it by checking whether str is a string and replacing any with unknown:

```
function splitChars(str: unknown) {
    if (typeof str === 'string') {
        return str.split('')
    }
    return []
}
```

Now the function returns an empty array [] as a fallback. It's an intentionally incorrect but technically valid result, as if the input was an empty string. It's a viable approach for secondary functions where correctness is less important than robustness. This is an example of what we described as graceful degradation in Chapter 1, Printing and Interpreting Errors, on page 1.

What if this function is in a mission-critical path, and a wrong result would mean data loss? Then you would prefer it to fail fast and loud rather than silently fall back.

```
function splitChars(str: unknown) {
    if (typeof str !== 'string') {
        throw new Error('')
    }
    return str.split('')
}
```

Now you can be sure that if the input is a string, you'll get a correct result. If it's something else, the program will let you know.

This works well but looks not so clean. These checks distract when reading, and in the core parts of a large application you want many of them, especially when working closely with external APIs. Instead of putting an if condition in every function, we can implement a small utility function similar to the assert utility in Node.js, but type-safe. We'll use TypeScript's operator asserts for that:

```
/**
    this utility is type-safe in compile time because of the usage of asserts
    and in runtime because this function actually checks the type of the value
*/
function assertIsString(val: any): asserts val is string {
  if (typeof val !== "string") {
    throw new Error("Not a string!");
  }
}
```

Now we can clean up the function body of splitChars:

```
function splitChars(str: unknown) {
    assertIsString(str)
    return str.split('') // No error! Typescript is sure this is a string now
}
```

It's often handy to have a more general assert utility in your codebase:

```
/**
    this utility is type-safe in compile time because of the usage of asserts
    and in runtime too, because this function really checks the type of the value
*/
function assert(claim: unknown, message="Assertion failed"): asserts claim {
  if (!claim) throw new Error(message);
}
```

Then you can use it, for example, to make sure an array item exists in both type-safe and runtime-safe ways:

```
const item = arr.shift() // can be undefined for empty arrays
assert(item)
item.doSomething() // typescript knows item is defined
```

You can use runtime assertions to ensure there's a field in a Record, and TypeScript's type inference will immediately figure out what type level the field exists on.

```
assert(userData["login"])
getUserConnections(userData["login"])
```

Runtime assertions with type inference are much better for runtime safety than using the non-null assertion operator ! or type assertions like as string. Runtime assertions will throw in both production and test environments, shifting the verification burden one level below even unit tests. The type inference will assure the claim is true even before you get to run the code, shifting part of the code validation further left.

Runtime assertions serve as a form of in-code documentation. They describe theoretical states that are allowed and ones that are not. You can think about assertions as self-checking code comments that never become outdated.

Assertions help you validate a simple statement in both type-safe and runtime-safe ways—for example, that a value exists, or a value is of a particular type, or that it's an instance of a class. If the statement is false, throw an exception. What if you want to validate a more complex statement that doesn't fit well into one condition, or make the code execution conditional depending on the variable type and make TypeScript understand it as well? Try type guards.

Fail Faster with Type Guards

Imagine you want to authenticate a user, and you have two functions to do that, depending on whether you have a valid user record at hand:

```
function login(user: User) {
    // triggers the login flow for the user
}

function register() {
    // triggers registration flow
}
```

For example, if you want to run two different procedures depending on whether the value is `null`, you can implement the following check:

```
/** Check if obj is null */
function isNull(obj: unknown): obj is null {
  return obj === null;
}
```

Then use it like this:

```
function authenticate(user: User | null) {
    if (isNull(user)) {
        register()
    } else {
        login(user)
    }
}
```

By calling `login(user)`, both you and TypeScript know that `user` is not `null`.

I'll use an example borrowed from Adam Coster[1] where he checks if an object is a duck. The simplest option is to use an instanceof condition.

```
if (thing instanceof Duck) {
    thing.quack()
}
```

This will work only if the thing has been created from the Duck constructor. What if it wasn't, and you still want to check if the object is a duck, defined as "a thing that can quack"? Then you can use type guards using TypeScript's is operator. First, we'll check if a thing is an object, if it has the field quack, and then if the field quack is a function.

```
/** Check if a value is a non-null object */
function isObject<T>(value:any): value is Exclude<object,null> {
  return value && typeof value === 'object';
}

/** Check if an object is a function */
function isFunction(obj: unknown): obj is () => unknown {
  return typeof obj === 'function';
}

/** Check if an object has a particular field */
function hasField<F extends string>(
    obj: unknown,
    field: F
): obj is Record<F, unknown> {
  return isObject(obj) && field in obj;
}

function isADuck(maybeDuck: any): maybeDuck is Duck {
  return hasField(maybeDuck, 'quack') && isFunction(maybeDuck.quack);
}
```

Only if all three conditions are true, we come to the conclusion: the thing in front of us is a duck, and we call .quack().

```
if (isADuck(thing)) {
    thing.quack()
}
```

Note that a function having is on its return type must return boolean.

Combine Type Guards with Assertions

Assertions and type guards perfectly complement each other, and TypeScript even allows you to use both asserts and is on the function return type:

```
function assertIsDuck(
```

1. https://adamcoster.com/blog/typescript-assertions-guards-narrowing

```
    maybeDuck: any,
    message="Not a duck!"
): asserts maybeDuck is Duck {
    assert(isADuck(maybeDuck))
}

assertIsDuck(thing)
thing.quack()
```

Use never Type

Type never is an underused tool in the arsenal of a TypeScript programmer. You normally see never in error messages, and usually it indicates that you got your type definitions wrong. However, you can use it intentionally to make code safer.

never as a return type means that the function never returns. For example, it always throws, like in code on page 65, or goes into an infinite loop.

```
function assertNever(x: never): never {
  throw new Error("Unexpected object: " + x);
}

function handleEvent(event: string | number) {
  switch (typeof event) {
    case "string":
      console.log("String event");
      break;
    case "number":
      console.log("Number event");
      break;
    default:
      assertNever(event);
  }
}
```

Instead of assertNever you could just use throw, but the explicit usage of never will cause the TypeScript interpreter to show an error when the event is anything but never. In other words, it will show an error when a value is used where it should not be theoretically possible.

```
function handleEvent(event: string | number) {
  switch (typeof event) {
    case "string":
      console.log("String event");
      break;
    default:
      assertNever(event); // TypeScript error, event can be "number" yet.
  }
}
```

This way you delegate validation from a runtime exception to the TypeScript interpreter which notifies you of a mistake before you run the code. Shift left.

Graceful Degradation

Noncritical, optional parts of an application can benefit from graceful degradation more than from failing fast. The two pillars of graceful degradation are fallback and retry.

Fallback is a plan B for when plan A fails. For example, if a thing that was supposed to be a duck cannot quack, ask a reserve duck:

```
// fallquack.ts
const fallbackDuck = new Duck()

// fallback quack
export function fallQuack() {
    fallbackDuck.quack()
}
```

Then use it as a reserve quack machine:

```
// main.ts
import {fallQuack} from './fallquack'

if (isADuck(thing)) {
    thing.quack()
} else {
    // if the thing can not quack, let the fallback duck quack
    fallQuack()
}
```

One common practical example of the fallback approach is polyfill. Polyfill is a piece of code used to provide modern functionality on older browsers that do not natively support it.

```
if (!Array.prototype.includes) {
    Array.prototype.includes = function(searchElement, fromIndex) {
        if (this == null) {
            throw new TypeError('"this" is null or not defined');
        }

        var o = Object(this);
        var len = o.length >>> 0;

        if (len === 0) {
            return false;
        }

        var n = fromIndex | 0;
        var k = Math.max(n >= 0 ? n : len - Math.abs(n), 0);

        while (k < len) {
```

```
            if (o[k] === searchElement) {
                return true;
            }
            k++;
        }
        return false;
    };
}
```

If a browser supports Array.includes, we use the native implementation because it's the most performant, well tested, and reliable. If not, we use our own implementation that does exactly the same thing.

The second pillar of graceful degradation is retry. If an operation fails, we make another attempt. This is especially useful in HTTP fetch requests.

```
async function retryWithBackoff<T>(
    operation: () => Promise<T>,
    maxAttempts: number = 5,
    initialDelay: number = 1000,
): Promise<T> {
    let attempt = 0;
    let delay = initialDelay;

    while (attempt < maxAttempts) {
        try {
            return await operation();
        } catch (error) {
            attempt += 1;
            if (attempt >= maxAttempts) {
                throw new Error(`
                    Operation failed after
                    ${maxAttempts} attempts.
                    Last error: ${error}
                `);
            }

            // Double the delay after each attempt
            delay *= 2;
            console.log(`Attempt ${attempt} failed. Retrying in ${delay}ms...`);

            // Wait for the calculated delay
            await new Promise(resolve => setTimeout(resolve, delay));
        }
    }

    throw new Error('Operation failed after maximum attempts');
}

retryWithBackoff(fetchData)
    .then(data => console.log('Success:', data))
    .catch(error => console.error('Failed after retries:', error));
```

Graceful degradation is good for end-user experience because it improves the perceived quality of the software, but it's rather harmful during development because it masks problems from you just as well as from end users. Once you have both graceful degradation and runtime assertion in your toolkit, you can combine them to make your program shout loud during development and put a good face on in production using debug runtime assertion.

Debug Runtime Assertion

How do you make your program behave differently during development and in production? The common convention is to use the `NODE_ENV` environment variable with the values `development`, `production`, and `test`, although you can use other values just as well if you have other environments. The variable is accessible in Node.js via `process.env.NODE_ENV` alongside other environment variables accessible via `process.env.VARIABLE_NAME`.

If you're using Vite to build your app, you can directly read from built-in Boolean constants `import.meta.env.PROD` and `import.meta.env.DEV`.

```
if (import.meta.env.PROD) {
    // production-only code
}

if (import.meta.env.DEV) {
    // development-only code
}
```

Now, in addition to a graceful degradation fallback, you can use an assertion that will throw only in the development environment using the environment variables.

```
function softAssert(condition: boolean, message: string) {
    if (!condition) {
        if (import.meta.env.DEV) {
            // Throw error in development
            throw new Error(message);
        } else {
            // Log warning in production
            console.warn(`Assertion failed: ${message}`);
        }
    }
}
```

Ship with Confidence

One of the reasons why we—developers—are so notoriously bad at time estimation is that when we estimate, we focus on implementation too much and pay too little attention to shipping. After all, implementation is our primary

Using Environment Variables with Webpack

If you're not using Vite but another build system—for example, webpack—you'll have to explicitly set environment variables. The simplest way is to do that directly in the npm scripts in the package.json of your project:

```
{
    "scripts": {
        "start":
            "NODE_ENV=development webpack serve --mode development --open",
        "build":
            "NODE_ENV=production webpack --mode production"
    }
}
```

Then define plugin in webpack.config.js:

```
const webpack = require('webpack');
module.exports = {
    // Other configuration settings...
    plugins: [
        new webpack.DefinePlugin({
            'process.env.NODE_ENV':
                JSON.stringify(process.env.NODE_ENV || 'development')
        })
    ]
};
```

After that, you can read the value in your client code:

```
if (process.env.NODE_ENV === "production") {
    // production-only code
}
if (process.env.NODE_ENV === "development") {
    // development-only code
}
```

job, and, in theory, if our primary job is done well, shipping must be a matter of merging a PR and waiting for it to deploy. Of course, this is just in theory. Reality hits as soon as the shipping day comes, and we get swamped by merge conflicts, feature inconsistencies, and bug reports. The good news is that it's not inevitable—you have a tested methodology that makes the shipping predictable.

Ship gradually, starting from a manually controlled feature gate. Then enable the feature gate to internal users (a practice known as dogfooding, coming from the "eat your own dogfood" idiom). Then ship to beta testers, a small group of external early adopters who want to see the latest improvements first and be in direct contact with you at the expense of seeing occasional imperfections. After the beta stage is finished, you can enable the flag for a gradually increasing share of users, starting from very small (0.1%–10%, depending on the size of your user base).

You'll notice that this process significantly differs from "merge into main and pick the next task from the backlog." Of course, not every feature has to go through the whole process. If your company is small and consists primarily of developers, then feature gating and dogfooding are essentially the same thing and can be merged. When your product has only 10 users, then beta testing and canary testing make little sense. Also, you may want to skip parts of the process for simple, straightforward features, and that's okay. Use your best judgment. The main benefit of this process is that you get issues reported in small chunks, and you fix them before they hit larger and more sensitive groups of users.

Feature Gating

The basis of any shipping process is feature gating. Switching any feature on must be as easy as flipping one flag from `false` to `true`, and roll-back should be just as easy. You can find powerful, advanced, feature-rich third-party services to manage feature flags, but their maintenance costs time and money and increases system complexity, so you shouldn't consider integrating them unless the primitive solution stops satisfying your needs.

Speaking about the primitive solution, you can cover many use cases in a tiny amount of code, so let's implement one together in this section, applying the tools we've covered earlier in this chapter. We'll start with a simple feature gate and build on that:

```
// is-feature-enabled.ts
const features = {
    redButton: false,
}

export function isFeatureEnabled(name: keyof typeof features) {
    return features[name] ?? false
}
```

We can use it like this:

```
// button.ts
// ...
if (isFeatureEnabled("redButton")) {
    button.style.backgroundColor = "red"
}
```

Now you can flip the flag by changing one value from true to false and back. This can get you far, but it's inconvenient for everyone but developers, and it doesn't let you switch on and off from the browser without code modification.

One common way to flip feature flags is by using URL params. Let's modify our isFeatureEnabled function:

```
export function isFeatureEnabled(name: keyof typeof features) {
    const params = new URLSearchParams(window.location.search);
    const override = params.get(name)

    // accept values "on" and "off" of the url param, and ignore all other values
    if (override === "on") return true
    if (override === "off") return false

    return features[name]
}
```

Now, if you open the page with ?redButton=on, you get the red button.

Internal Testing

Just as we shifted bug discovery left during development, we shift it left at shipping time. Why wait until users find bugs if you can detect and fix them before release, with lower pressure? Your teammates and coworkers are your best testers. They know what the product is capable of and are motivated to write a good informative bug report and maybe even suggest a fix. Also, the price of making a mistake in front of your colleagues is low, and you won't have to run urgent hotfixes, so you can afford to be bold.

Let's expand our feature gating system to enable internal testing of experimental features. First, in place of one map features we'll create two: stableFeatures defining if a feature is enabled globally and internalFeatures defining if they are enabled for internal users:

```
const stableFeatures = {
    redButton: false,
}

const internalFeatures: Record<keyof typeof stableFeatures, boolean> = {
    redButton: true,
}
```

Then we'll modify our isFeatureEnabled function to take values from one or the other, depending on the environment:

```
export function isFeatureEnabled(name: keyof typeof stableFeatures) {
    const params = new URLSearchParams(window.location.search);
    const override = params.get(name)

    // accept values "on" and "off" of the url param, and ignore all other values
```

```
    if (override === "on") return true
    if (override === "off") return false

    // if there is an environment-specific override, return it
    if (import.meta.env.DEV && (name in internalFeatures)) {
        return internalFeatures[name]
    }

    return stableFeatures[name]
}
```

Now the feature redButton will be exposed to other developers using your product in the dev environment, allowing them to "eat their own dogfood" during development, or "drink their own champagne" if you prefer.

Beta Testing

Releasing a feature into beta is usually done in a similar manner. We create one more record with beta features:

```
const stableFeatures = {
    redButton: false,
    newSidebar: false,
}

const betaFeatures: Record<keyof typeof stableFeatures, boolean> = {
    newSidebar: true,
}

const internalFeatures: Record<keyof typeof stableFeatures, boolean> = {
    redButton: true,
}
```

Let's modify isFeatureEnabled to return beta features on staging:

```
export function isFeatureEnabled(name: keyof typeof stableFeatures) {
    const params = new URLSearchParams(window.location.search);
    const override = params.get(name)

    // accept values "on" and "off" of the url param, and ignore all other values
    if (override === "on") return true
    if (override === "off") return false

    // if there is an environment-specific override, return it
    if (import.meta.env.DEV && (name in internalFeatures)) {
        return internalFeatures[name]
    }

    if (import.meta.env.MODE === "staging" && (name in betaFeatures)) {
        return betaFeatures[name]
    }

    return stableFeatures[name]
}
```

This will work, given that your beta build is being run with the mode "staging," like this: `vite build --mode staging`.

Canary Tests and Gradual Rollout

Sometimes your change is in a fundamental part of the application, and its impact is so wide that it's practically impossible to fully test in isolation. Also, the leap between beta testing on dozens of users who are open to seeing imperfections and thousands of production users who expect top-grade quality is so wide that you don't want to cover it in one go. If you foresee potential problems affecting an unpredictable number of users, a common first step after the beta stage is canary testing.

Canary testing got its name after the historical practice of using canaries in coal mines to detect toxic gases. Coal miners would bring caged canary birds into the mines. Canaries have a lower tolerance to toxic gases, so when a canary stopped singing, it was a signal to get out of the mine.

Similarly, canary testing is when you release an update to a small group of users first to detect any issues before a wider rollout. Those users are normally unaware of being part of a test group, so for the canary test to be effective, you'll need a good monitoring system to track errors and match them with a test group. We'll talk about error monitoring in Chapter 8, Make Your Code Debuggable, on page 113.

For now, let's expand our feature gating system with a gradual rollout. After all, canary testing can be seen as a case of gradual rollout, but with a low sample size.

```
const gradualRollout: Record<keyof typeof stableFeatures, number> = {
    redButton: 0.01, // will be enabled for 1% of users
}

export function isFeatureEnabled(name: keyof typeof stableFeatures) {
    const params = new URLSearchParams(window.location.search);
    const override = params.get(name)

    // accept values "on" and "off" of the url param, and ignore all other values
    if (override === "on") return true
    if (override === "off") return false

    // if there is an environment-specific override, return it
    if (import.meta.env.DEV && (name in internalFeatures)) {
        return internalFeatures[name]
    }

    if (import.meta.env.MODE === "staging" && (name in betaFeatures)) {
        return betaFeatures[name]
    }
```

```
    // if gradual rollout is defined for a feature,
    // return true with the given probability
    if (name in gradualRollout) {
        return Math.random() < gradualRollout[name]
    }

    return stableFeatures[name]
}
```

This gradual rollout system is unstable, meaning that the same feature can be unpredictably enabled or disabled for the same user on every visit. Techniques exist to make them stable—namely, caching the result of gradual rollout evaluation in local storage or using a stable hash of the user ID instead of `Math.random`. They're usually tailored to specific needs (and are pretty fun to code), so we'll not be covering them in this book.

Do a Full-On Cleanup

After the feature has been staging for enough time (be it on alpha, beta, or gradual rollout), you want to do two consecutive things: roll it out to 100% of users and clean it up.

The full release looks like this:

```
const stableFeatures = {
    redButton: true,
}
```

Usually, you want to give the feature some cool-down period after going full-on before cleaning everything up, to keep the door open to urgently switching `true` back to `false`. No universal rules declare how long you should keep it, nor how long a feature should be in staging. I've seen people use hours, and I've seen months. You'll have to decide for yourself, depending on the feature, the product, and current business priorities.

We've just implemented a small and flexible feature gating system in 50 lines of code. You might be wondering: if it's so easy, why isn't everyone doing it? I don't have an answer. We all should be.

Keep Moving in a Data-Driven Company

Some companies, mostly established corporations past the age of moving fast, learn to love A/B testing. The first months and even years of A/B testing on a product can be fun: you come up with bright ideas, you set up experiments, you measure impact, and you win. Then gradually, little by little, you run out of easy wins, and fun fades away.

During my time at Booking.com, A/B tests were mandatory. Every change, even a minor tooltip rephrasing or a cosmetic improvement, had to conclusively bring more cash—for example, increase hotel reservations or decrease cancellations per day. The company let us be more flexible with bugfixes and demanded only that we show a statistically significant confirmation that the fix does not reduce cash flow.

A/B testing is an unbeaten tool for one thing: optimizing for a chosen metric toward its local optimum. A/B tests on their own never give answers on *why?* Why does conversion drop when you speed up page loading? Why has time spent on a page increased? The only honest answer to these questions starts with "I don't know for sure, but my guess is ..." A/B testing, similar to AI-assisted debugging, builds up intellectual debt. See Reduce Intellectual Debt, on page 49.

Frustratingly surprising was the fact that it was extremely hard to fix a minor bug without lowering conversion. The absolute worst is when a bug makes reality look better than it is—for example, it correctly displays that a hotel has a cafeteria but does not clearly state that it's closed. It's not illegal, but it's clearly unethical and almost impossible to fix without ruining conversion. Try convincing your boss that the company will start losing a whole team's salaries because of your change for the sake of ethics.

If you find yourself in such an environment and are not in a position to run away, brace yourself. The only way to not have a product full of these unfixable bugs is to not let them ever happen, and that is well within your control.

A/B tests take time. They require attention, maintenance, and frequent cleaning. They increase the cognitive load. Let it slip, and you find yourself staring at the editor, trying to make sense of stacked experiments, some poorly cleaned up and others abandoned forever. The product becomes fragile and unreadable.

Wrapping Up

In this chapter, you've learned design patterns and development practices to help you ship software of quality and with confidence. You've learned to configure Prettier and run it on a pre-commit hook; we've gone through the principles of clean code and the values behind them; and we've covered different types of automated testing. Finally, you've learned to make your code bulletproof by using runtime assertions and to ship with confidence using staging and gradual rollouts.

In the next chapter we'll cover how to deal with bugs that we couldn't prevent: you'll learn to observe the program state during execution, and we'll take a close look at interactive debugging in Chromium developer tools.

CHAPTER 6

Following the Data Flow

You're already familiar with the Sources panel in Developer Tools, but there's so much more to it than code listings and breakpoints. Unless you've intentionally and thoroughly learned to use the debugger, it's likely that you repeatedly use the same few capabilities, as I did for a long time: step in, step out, step forward, pause, and resume.

Beyond that is a whole underwater iceberg. The debugger allows you to conditionally stop execution. It allows you to stop on exceptions, page element modifications, and specific user events. It lets you watch expressions and run JavaScript snippets amid execution, among many other powerful things. In this chapter, you'll learn them all in practice.

To follow along with this chapter and get the most out of it, you'll need to clone and run the Pong game that we'll be using:

```
git clone https://github.com/oshibka404/pong.git
git switch 3-interactive
cd pong
yarn && yarn dev
```

In this chapter, you'll learn to navigate the call stack, control code execution flow, inspect values, watch expressions, and modify data in runtime. You'll get to create and use conditional breakpoints, DOM breakpoints, and log points, and you'll learn about front-end tooling that simplifies code navigation.

Defining What "Fixed" Means

After you start the game by running `yarn dev` and opening `localhost:3000` in a browser, you, as a player, will see a ping-pong table with a sign inviting you to press the space bar to start the game (as shown in the following image). But there's a problem—the game is already running. The ball is in motion, and the score is updated, but players don't have any control over the paddles yet. Press the space bar and see what happens. The game continues, allowing players to manipulate the paddles, but it doesn't reset the score. We have clear steps to reproduce the bug, and it consistently occurs. Let's fix it together.

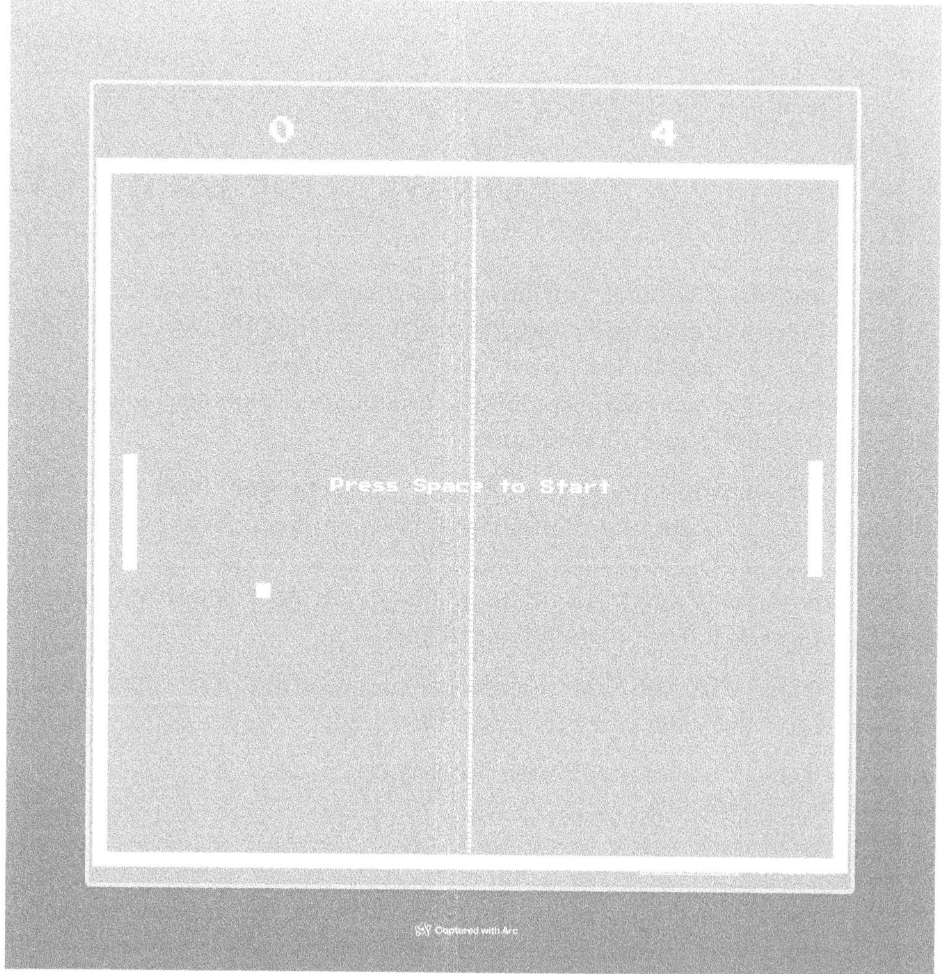

What does it mean to "fix it"? What should happen after you hit Start? Here are some options:

- The tennis table should not be visible at all until the player hits the space bar.
- The table should be visible with the ball standing still until the player presses the space bar.

- The gameplay should run in the background for illustration purposes and be reset on the space bar. If that's the case, then what?
  - Should the ball follow some specific trajectory (for instance, bounce strictly horizontally)?
  - Should the paddles be moving by themselves?
  - Should the paddles be moving when the user presses control keys?
  - Should the score update when the ball hits the goal line while running in the background?
  - Should the score be visible at all while the game is playing itself in the background?

Clarifying the Expected Behavior

In a business setting, the questions in the previous section are usually addressed to designers and product managers. When multiple parties are involved, it's important that everyone agrees on the definition of "fixed." It's even better when everyone explicitly agrees—better still, when everyone agrees in writing. If you're a one-person enterprise or working on a pet project, you get to decide what to do without worrying about other people, but even in such a case, you must clarify the expected behavior for yourself before you start. Speaking from my own experience, sometimes I don't know how unclear my expectations have been until I write them down, at least briefly.

For the rest of the chapter, we'll assume the following:

- Gameplay should be running in the background; it looks more fun and alive than a static picture.
- Paddles should not be moving until the player presses the space bar. They stay in the middle.
- When the player presses the space bar, the score is reset, the ball comes back to the center, and the game begins.

Following the same scientific method as discussed in Chapter 4, start with observation. Just by looking at the page, you might form some hypotheses, but the more evidence you gather, the more accurate your hypotheses will be. Look at the page, open the console, and reproduce the bug several times. Observation saves more time than it takes. If you find no clues during observation, that's important too. It means that you can exclude some of the hypotheses you've had.

Overcoming Blank Console Paralysis

The console is not helpful this time. It has no error messages referring to a particular line of code. In fact, it has no messages at all, so, unless you really know the codebase, it's not immediately clear where to start. This is the debugging equivalent of what writers call "blank-page paralysis"—a situation where you have a virtually infinite number of options, and to start, to make a leap from nothing to something, you have to choose only one. The advice people usually give sounds easy. Start from anywhere. It's okay to start from the wrong place because you can start again later at any time.

I'm Feeling Lucky

One way to "start from anywhere" is to halt execution at a random place and start exploring wherever you land. Staying on the Press Space to Start game screen with the developer tools panel open, go to the Sources panel and click the Pause Script Execution button. If your developer tools are in horizontal or detached mode, you'll find them on top of the right sidebar. Alternatively, you can press F8 on the keyboard (see the following image).

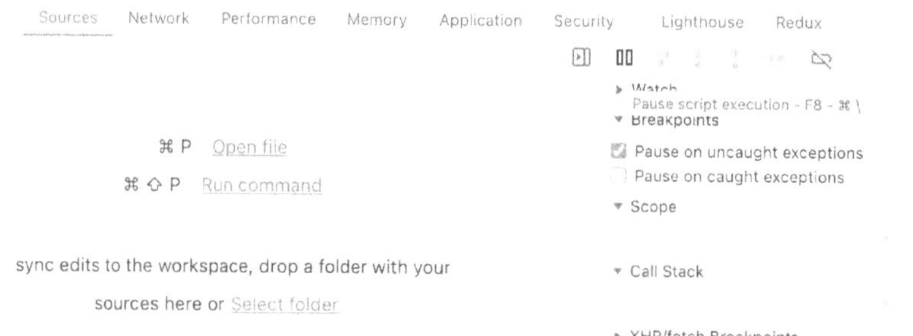

This method is a great starting point for debugging scripted animations, heavy long-running computations, repeatedly called operations (like in setInterval and recursive calls), and suspected infinite loops. It's not suitable for finding issues in scripts that are executed just once, because to land in a meaningful place, you need to pause execution at the moment when something meaningful is happening to have a chance to catch the bug red-handed.

Getting to Know the Sources Panel

In our case, after pausing execution, chances are that you ended up in the method called nextFrame. It's not the only possible place, just the most likely one. Try to press that button again to resume script execution, and then pause another time and yet one more time to find out what other processes are running, and follow along when the execution stops in nextFrame, as seen in this screenshot:

Like anything else ever written, code makes the most sense within a larger context. Every module is a part of a bigger system, and understanding a module is difficult without understanding the system at least on some level.

The File Tree

In the left panel, you find the file tree. The folder hierarchy overview shows where the module fits in the structure. From the path /pong/src/screens/-match/index.ts, you can conclude that you're seeing the file of a game screen called match of the pong game. So you're in the right place.

Note that every .ts file has a duplicate. It's a source map of the very same code transpiled to ES6, thus a little closer to what is being executed by the JavaScript engine. It comes in handy sometimes when, for instance, short TypeScript constructions like enum tend to generate longer JavaScript code and TypeScript source maps obscure the lower-level steps that are happening.

The Scope

In the right panel, under the Scope, you can find all the values available in the current moment of the script execution process. They're categorized in three buckets:

- *Local scope:* Variables within the current function or code block.
- *Module scope:* Values declared on the top level or imported into the current module.
- *Global scope:* Properties of the global Window object.

Usually, the local and module-wide scopes are the most relevant ones you use to get familiar with the surroundings.

In our case, the local scope has only one variable, elapsedTime, so you can conclude the method does calculations depending on the moment in time, which is typical for animations. Also, note that the type of execution context, this, is annotated as Match. Feel free to expand it and explore its properties.

The module context offers more food for thought. It has, among others, defaultModelState and MatchOverlay. This might initially seem insignificant, but here are only some of the conclusions you might draw observing that:

- The defaultModelState.gameplayTime has a nonzero value that doesn't look like a default one, and this value updates every time you pause and unpause execution. It means that the state object is mutable. It's not bad per se and is widespread in game development, but it can cause trouble. In some frameworks, such as React, the mutable state is considered an antipattern.
- The defaultModelState.status equals 'not_started' and the ball is moving, so the gameplay must be controlled by something else. Possibly, mistakenly.
- The name MatchOverlay next to MatchTable looks like a class representing an element covering the match table, so you might want to explore that as well.

The Call Stack

The Call Stack can be found in the same right panel as the scope. It usually provides useful system knowledge, as we'll see later in this chapter. If you expand it and scroll down a little, you'll see that the function nextFrame is repeatedly calling itself using requestAnimationFrame (see the following image). It's a common pattern of requestAnimationFrame usage, so it's nothing special. But taking into account that the method name is nextFrame and its argument is elapsedTime, you can be confident that you're observing a method asynchronously computing and drawing an animation frame based on a moment in time.

You might be wondering why I spend so much time talking about context and only now get to the code itself, the core of a programmer's work. You may argue that most of the time, you don't need to learn about other modules to find and fix a particular issue, and I agree on that point. However, there are good reasons to still do it. The first is learning. Through debugging and close inspection, you can and will see places you wouldn't find otherwise. I've been in countless situations when a look at context before diving into code not only benefited me long-term or had educational value but also helped me find the issue faster because I noted something odd in the surrounding values. And to notice that something is odd, you need to know what normal looks like. So, observe closely; observe repeatedly. And with that said, let's jump into the code.

Navigating the Code

When the code execution is on pause, the debugger evaluates all expressions in the current function scope down to the current pause point. You can see their values next to each line where they're referenced (see line 57 in the screenshot). Hover over a class or variable name, and you'll see its value in a tooltip. It can be local, module, or a globally defined symbol, but note that you'll see only values that are declared in a scope visible from the current point in execution.

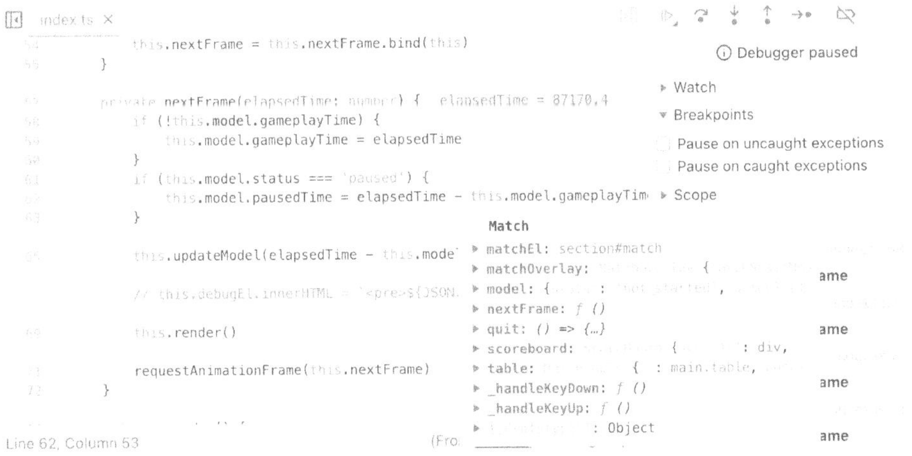

Debugger can only see values that are currently in memory, which means that you won't see things the garbage collector has already removed from RAM, even if they should be available—for instance, via closure.

While the execution is still paused on the first line of the method (line 58), right-click line 65 and Continue to Here in the context menu. Note that line 65 is now highlighted and the expressions are evaluated.

Inspect the Code Using the Console

Press Escape on the keyboard. The already familiar console opens below. You can use it to inspect the values during the execution.

Type `elapsedTime` and press Enter. Type `this.` (including the period after). Browse through autocompletion to see what properties are available in the current execution context (see the following image).

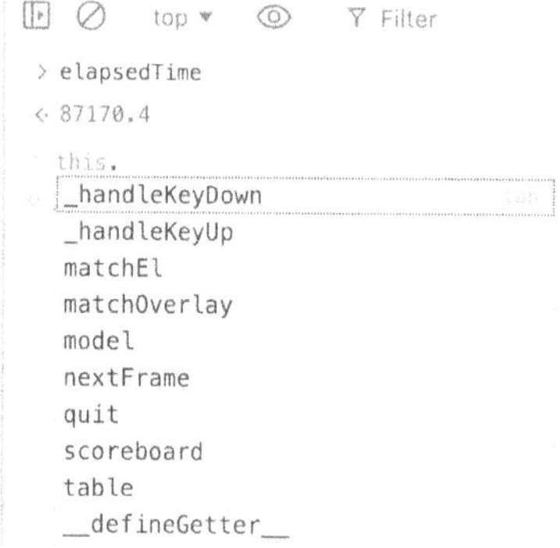

Choose `matchOverlay` from the dropdown and press Tab to autocomplete. Type `.` (a period) to see its field list. Note that you see even the fields that are declared as `private` in TypeScript—for example, `matchOverlay.matchStateMessageEl` and `matchOverlay.quit`. Choose `quit` from the dropdown list of properties and press Enter. The method's listing will appear.

Being able to inspect `private` properties is a powerful tool in debugging. However, it means that those properties are not truly private, and code consumers can abuse them and use private methods in runtime by overriding TypeScript warnings, which is another common source of bugs that are hard to find. You should never use as `public` what is declared `private`, and if you find others doing so, either remove such usages or make the method signatures explicitly `public`.

Note that you cannot see properties declared using the # prefix in debugger this way. Those are truly private and can be accessed only from the class where they are defined. Also, it's super common that with source maps, variables that you see in code listing are not available in the console. For instance, `import { member } from "module"` sometimes gets transformed into `_module.member`, and naively typing `member` in the console will result in a `ReferenceError`. A work-around for this is to toggle source maps off by pressing Cmd+Shift+P in Chrome developer tools and check the actual JavaScript code being executed.

Stepping in a Stepwise Execution

Next to Resume Execution in the right panel, find Step into Next Function Call (↓) (see the following image). Press it while on the line with the this.updateModel call.

You'll find yourself on the first line of the same class's updateModel method. Press the second button in the row, Step over Next Function Call (↷) (see the next image).

You'll move the execution to the next line and see the timeDelta value calculated.

Run JS Snippets During Execution

Now, for the beautiful part: you can change values on the run! Type timeDelta = 100 in the debugging console and step forward one more time, then step into this.table.updateModel(timeDelta) by pressing ↓. You'll find yourself in a different file, table.ts, in a function that updates the model of the tennis table. Notice that its input argument, timeDelta, is equal to 100, as you specified it.

You can run any JavaScript the same way right in the middle of execution, even DOM modifications, and even perform network requests. Feel free to run something like document.body.style.backgroundColor = 'red' and immediately see the background color updated.

Watch Expressions

Find and expand Watch in the right sidebar. Press the Add Watch Expression (+) button and add some expressions you want to observe, ball.position and ball.speed. It's useful to know that you can use not only values but any executable expressions, which will be reevaluated at every step. For instance, if you wanted to know how far the ball is from the center, you could add the watch expression Math.sqrt(ball.position.x ** 2 + ball.position.y ** 2) (see the image that follows).

```
▼ Watch                          + ↻
▼ ball.speed: Object
    x: -1
    y: 0.26854312244725964
  ▶ [[Prototype]]: Object
▼ ball.position: Object
    x: -25100.1274
    y: 6740.466585820017
  ▶ [[Prototype]]: Object
```

Step through the function using Step Over and explore how these values change and what code branches are executed. Note what changes are expected to happen to the table tennis contents in 100 milliseconds (because we deliberately set timeDelta to 100).

The MatchTable.updateModel method calculates and updates values in the local tennis table model, which contains the coordinates and speed of the ball and paddles.

You've found out that Match.updateModel updates a local model and triggers an update of its children by calling MatchTable.updateModel. You've learned what each model has and what real values appear there. Let's move on.

Navigating the Call Stack

Look at the call stack (see the image that follows). Note that you're two levels deeper than nextFrame, where you landed initially (remember, you pressed ↓ twice).

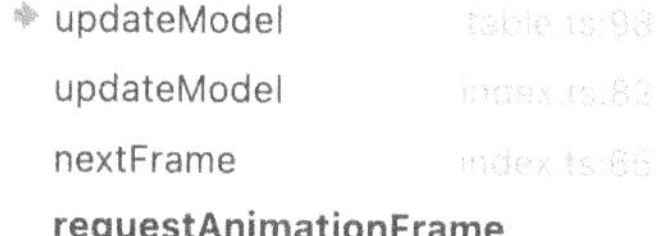

Click other items in the call stack. It won't affect execution, but you can inspect the code at every level of the call tree. You won't be able to watch expressions or execute commands on levels other than the top one unless you step out of it.

In the row of the execution control buttons, find and press Step Out of the Current Function (↑) twice to go back to nextFrame.

You'll end up on the next executable line inside nextFrame, which is the call to this.render(). Feel free to step into it and see what it does. It calls the render method on the screen children, which updates the visual elements according to the models we updated earlier.

```
private render() {
        this.table.render()
        this.scoreboard.render()
}
```

Now you can execute the application step-by-step, going deeper if you need. We've covered observation and navigation; let's figure out what precedes the start of animation and how we can change it.

Storing Values as Global Variables

A true hidden gem of Chrome developer tools is storing values as global variables. While staying on the breakpoint in nextFrame, type in the console this.model and press Enter. Right-click the logged object and choose Store as Global Variable (see the following image).

It will be stored as temp1. Now, in the right sidebar, click Deactivate Breakpoints and resume execution (see the next image).

Deactivate breakpoints - ⌘ F8

The game goes on. The match model that is normally stored in a private property of a class becomes available for your manipulation.

Type temp1.status = 'paused'. Now you can programmatically pause and unpause the game while it's running in the background, as well as unstart it by setting it back to 'not_started', which wouldn't be possible from the UI under any circumstances.

Using Breakpoints

Of the nine breakpoint types, in this chapter you'll touch the line-of-code, column-in-line, DOM, event listener, and conditional breakpoints, as well as log points. We'll consider XHR breakpoints in Chapter 7, Debugging Asynchronous Operations, on page 99, and we've discussed the exception breakpoints in Chapter 1, Printing and Interpreting Errors, on page 1. The ninth type, the trusted type breakpoint, is useful for XSS protection, and you can find it discussed in the Chrome DevTools documentation.

First, let's find out what triggers the initial animation by seeing where nextFrame is first called. In our scenario, triggering the animation could be as simple as Cmd+clicking the method signature in the IDE and manually navigating through the three method references. However, in real-world scenarios where a function is used in hundreds of places, and you want to investigate its call in a specific case, breakpoints in the debugger serve as an ideal tool.

Line-of-Code Breakpoints

Set a breakpoint on the first line of the nextFrame method. To do that, left-click a number to the left from the line `if (!this.model.gameplayTime) {`. You'll see a small blue arrow representing the breakpoint (as shown the following screenshot). Refresh the page and press Start in the main menu.

We're back in nextFrame. Expand the call stack in the right sidebar. Below the already familiar requestAnimationFrame, you'll see a sequence of calls that led us here. Take your time to click through them and look at what triggered the animation. What other calls preceded or followed the animation's start? If you discover a method that allows us to easily reset the score and start the game, we can use it to fix the bug.

The first stop in the call stack is setStatus. It's short and rather clear. It sets the current match status to the model and either hides or shows the matchOverlay, then triggers the first animation frame.

```
private setStatus(status: MatchStatus) {
        this.model.status = status
        if (status === 'running') {
                this.matchOverlay.hide()
        } else {
                this.matchOverlay.show(status)
        }
        requestAnimationFrame(this.nextFrame)
}
```

So far, so good. If we wanted to disable animation until the user hits the space bar to start the match, we would just move the requestAnimationFrame(this.nextFrame) call into the same branch where we hide the overlay, like this:

```
private setStatus(status: MatchStatus) {
        this.model.status = status
        if (status === 'running') {
                this.matchOverlay.hide()
                requestAnimationFrame(this.nextFrame)
        } else {
                this.matchOverlay.show(status)
        }
}
```

It's not what we want, but trying it out to verify that it works is a wise thing to do. In case you cannot come up with the desired solution in a reasonable time, it's highly professional to have an alternative fix prepared. Feel free to go to IDE and change that line, then save, refresh the page, and check if the animation isn't started until the player hits the space bar. Then undo the change, and we'll continue our search for the desired solution.

Step one more call up to Match.show.

```
show() {
        this.matchEl.style.display = 'flex'
        this.table.init({
                width: this.matchEl.clientWidth,
                height: this.matchEl.clientHeight
        })
        this.initKeyboard()
>>>>this.setStatus('not_started')
        this.table.reset()
}
```

It does several things: it sets style.display property of matchEl, which seems to be the game screen, initializes the keyboard and the table itself, and then sets the match status to 'not_started' and resets the table.

this.table.reset() looks like a potentially useful line. We want to reset the table on the space bar. Let's check if it does what we expect it to do. Add a breakpoint on it, refresh the page, and step into the function.

```
reset() {
        this.model.ball = {
                position: {x: 0, y: 0},
                speed: {x: 0, y: 0}
        }

        setTimeout(() => {
                this.model.ball.speed.x = Math.random() > .5 ? -1 : 1
                this.model.ball.speed.y = Math.random()
        }, 1000)
}
```

Yes, it puts the ball in the middle and throws it in after a timeout. Let's find where we should call it.

Column-in-Line Breakpoints

When multiple function calls are happening on the same line, the debugger allows you to set a breakpoint on one or more of the calls, which are commonly called columns, as opposed to lines. To try it out in the current file, got to constructor of the Match class and set a breakpoint on this.scoreboard.onWin(() => { (see the following image).

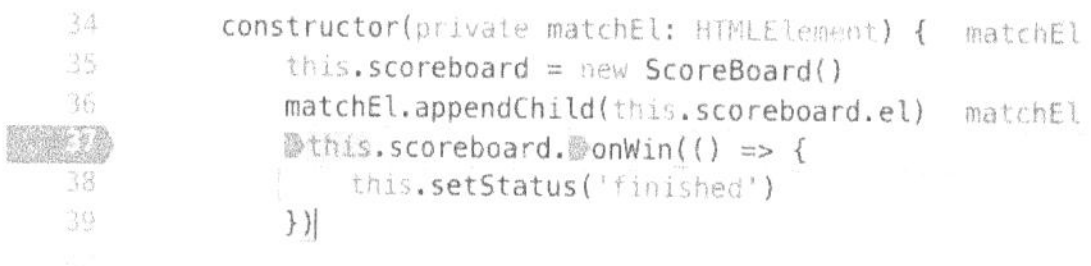

DOM Breakpoints

Click the Select an Element to Inspect button. In the top-left corner of the developer tools, select the Press Space to Start overlay.

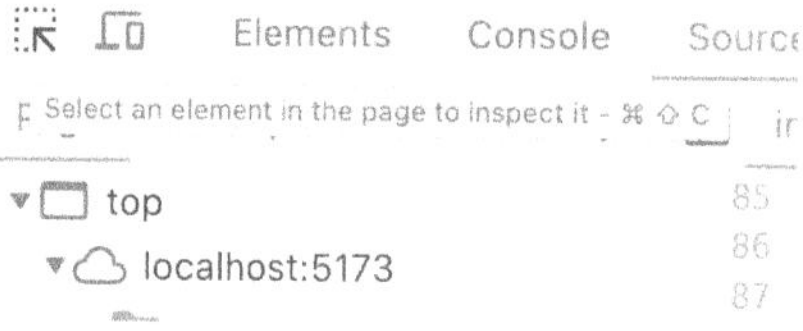

You switched to the Elements panel, and the element with class `match-state` should be selected. Right-click it and select Break On > Attribute Modifications (see the next screenshot).

Go back to the Sources tab and expand the DOM Breakpoints section in the right sidebar. You should see a new breakpoint.

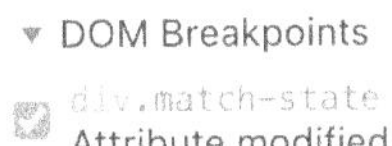

Disable by unchecking checkboxes for the old line-of-code breakpoints, or just delete them to not get distracted.

Breakpoints
Pause on uncaught exceptions
Pause on caught exceptions
index.ts
58
scoreboard.ts
32

Now, click Resume Execution ( ) and press the space bar to start the game.

You should land in the method called `MatchOverlay.hide`, on the line where the overlay's `display` style is set to `none`, thus visually hiding it. Study the stack trace. This is the sequence of calls happening at the moment when the overlay closes. We might want to add the logic. We see the already familiar `setStatus`, which is, in order, called from a method called `startGame`.

```
private startGame() {
        this.setStatus('running')
}
```

This seems to be precisely what we're looking for, and now we know empirically where it's called from and in which real, not hypothetical, context.

Event Listener Breakpoints

Another way to find this method would be to see what handles the space bar press. Find the section called Event Listener Breakpoints in the right sidebar, and find keydown and keypress events in it (see the following image). Then resume execution and hit that space bar.

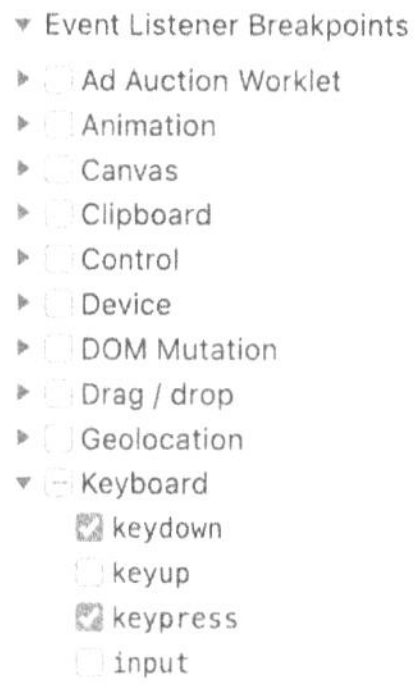

```
▼ Event Listener Breakpoints
  ▶ ☐ Ad Auction Worklet
  ▶ ☐ Animation
  ▶ ☐ Canvas
  ▶ ☐ Clipboard
  ▶ ☐ Control
  ▶ ☐ Device
  ▶ ☐ DOM Mutation
  ▶ ☐ Drag / drop
  ▶ ☐ Geolocation
  ▼ ☐ Keyboard
      ☑ keydown
      ☐ keyup
      ☑ keypress
      ☐ input
```

You'll land in the event listener.

```
}
              "Space"
private handleKeydown(e: KeyboardEvent) {   e = KeyboardEvent {isTrus
    switch (e.code) {
        case 'Space':
            if (this.model.status === 'running') {
                this.setStatus('paused')
            } else if (this.model.status === 'not_started') {
                this.startGame()
            } else if (this.model.status === 'paused') {
                this.setStatus('running')
            }
            break;
        case 'Escape':
```

Then, following the code execution, you'll find that the startGame is called. You came to the same place from the opposite side of the call stack.

Conditional Breakpoints

One more, perhaps more elegant, way of finding the call sequence leading to the game start would be to go to the Match.setStatus method and set a conditional breakpoint on its first line.

Right-click the line number next to the first line of the method and choose Add Conditional Breakpoint.... Alternatively, you can take a regular breakpoint, right-click it, and choose Edit Breakpoint; then switch it to conditional.

Type in the field status === 'running' && this.model.status === 'not_started' (see the following image). Now the execution will stop on this line of code if and only if the match status changes from not_started to running.

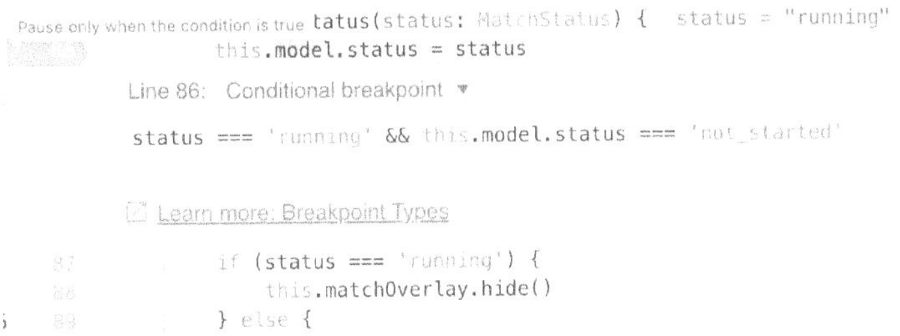

Then do the same familiar routine of following the breadcrumbs of the call stack until you notice something relevant.

Log Points

While you're on this line, try switching it from Conditional Breakpoint to Logpoint and type:

```
`going from ${this.model.status} to ${status}`
```

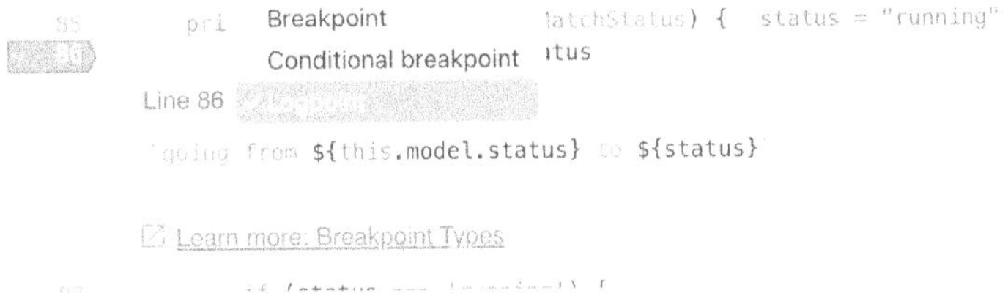

This is the way to add log values without modifying code in the IDE. This way, you definitely won't forget to delete console statements from the code before deploying it. Log points are extremely useful when code modifications cause rebuilds that can last a significant amount of time, so going to the IDE and adding console.log statements everywhere is not a possible option. Also, you can switch less between browser and IDE, thus reducing the cognitive load.

Now, switch to IDE and modify this method:

```
private startGame() {
        this.setStatus('running')
        this.table.reset()
}
```

Refresh the page and start the game to check if the ball is returning to the center on the space bar now. It is. Great! Now, we want to reset the score.

Remember that render method that updated element views based on just-updated models? It called this.table.render() and this.scoreboard.render(). Put a breakpoint into it, and hover over this.scoreboard to see if a method to reset its value is available (see the image that follows).

We're lucky this time! There's a method called reset. Check if it does what we need:

```
reset() {
        this.model.p1 = 0
        this.model.p2 = 0
}
```

Change the startGame method:

```
private startGame() {
        this.setStatus('running')
        this.table.reset()
        this.scoreboard.reset()
}
```

Verify that the bug is fixed. It is! Now, let's make the fix better.

Improving the Fix

> If we all checked in our code a little cleaner than when we checked it out, the code simply could not rot.
>
> ➤ *Robert C. Martin, Clean Code*

According to *Clean Code*, a function should do one thing and operate on only one level of abstraction. Let's extract resetting components to a separate reset method and call it.

```
private startGame() {
        this.setStatus('running')
```

```
        this.reset()
}

private reset() {
        this.table.reset()
        this.scoreboard.reset()
}
```

Now you've solved a problem and improved the code. It's a bugfix done right; you can be proud of yourself.

Using Source Maps

Be prepared that in reality it won't always be that easy. Some building tools will show you a flat list of files instead of a hierarchy. Some source maps won't support column breakpoints or will consistently stop execution on a different line than the one you set a breakpoint on. Sometimes they'll show you the whole bundle as one single code listing, and sometimes you'll have to debug minified JavaScript without any source maps at all. You can make it more manageable, though. For example, to find a file in an endless list of project files or in a complex project hierarchy, you can press Cmd+P (Ctrl+P on Windows or Linux) and start typing the file name (see the following image).

To make minified code more readable, you can use the Pretty Print button, and it will automatically format the code with line breaks and indentations.

The image at the top of the next page shows some code before and after using Pretty Print.

If you have some influence in your organization, and it seems possible under your circumstances, you should invest in a better front-end infrastructure. As you can now clearly see, good source maps and hot module replacement simplify development a lot, and, just like with any technical debt, the earlier you deal with it, the easier it will be.

Disabling Source Maps

Source maps are a big topic of their own, and in this chapter we'll cover only a couple of techniques useful for interactive debugging. If your source maps are working poorly, or you suspect that a transpiler, or a minifier, rather than a programmer's mistake, is causing your bug, and you wish to debug the actual JavaScript code the browser is executing, disable source maps. Go to the developer tools settings (the ⚙ button in the top-right corner) and turn off the JavaScript Source Maps checkbox under the Sources category, as shown in the following image.

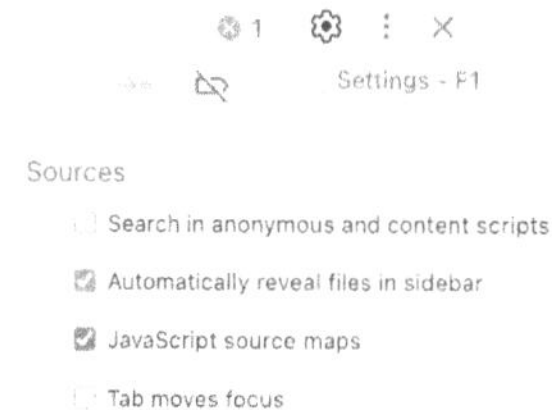

Using an Ignore List

Debugging an application that heavily uses a library like Lodash or jQuery or a framework like React or Vue, you usually want to focus on the code of your application rather than the library code. However, library internals tend to pollute the call stack to the degree that you can't find anything meaningful. The same applies to in-house libraries, which are common in large products.

To exclude a script from the call stack in developer tools, right-click it in the code browser and select Add Script to Ignore List in the context menu (see the following image). This operation is also commonly known as blackboxing because ignore-listed parts of the codebase become “black boxes”: entities of which we know inputs and outputs, but know nothing about their internals.

You can edit the list of currently ignore-listed by going to the DevTools Settings (⚙) and switching to Ignore List in the left sidebar, as seen in the next image.

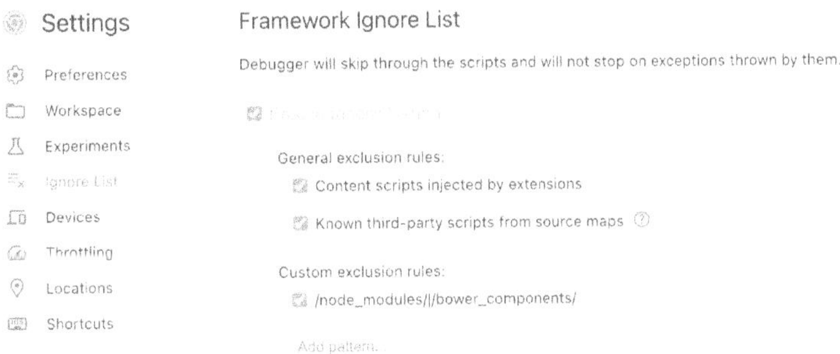

Alternatively, use the ignoreList source map extension so that it will be black-boxed for everyone using the project. Depending on the build system, the process varies slightly. To give you an example, in Vite, to add all contents of node_modules to an ignore list, you can add the following property to the object exported from vite.config.js:

```
rollupOptions: {
        sourcemapIgnoreList: (relativeSourcePath, sourcemapPath) => {
                return relativeSourcePath.includes('node_modules');
        },
}
```

The debugger Statement

If you can avoid the `debugger` statement, do so. The `debugger` statement is a way to halt code execution right from your source code. Executed in a browser with DevTools open, the code will stop on a `debugger` statement, as if there was a breakpoint. The only time it makes sense to use it is during interactive debugging of minified code without source maps, when you're unable to locate a function by its name or contents.

Wrapping Up

After completing this chapter, you should be able to do the following:

- Control code execution: move forward, inside and outside functions; pause execution conditionally; pause it on DOM modifications and on events fired.
- Read and use the call stack to trace the path leading to the current execution point.
- Watch expressions and print values without code modification, using log points.
- Run JavaScript snippets during debugging and inspect runtime values using the console.
- Use source maps, configure and disable them, and use an ignore list locally and via tool configuration.

Bonus Exercise

- Remember that `defaultModelState` didn't look very default-like and turned out to be mutable? Find a bug caused by it. Do you see how to fix it?
- The game keeps running in the background when you reach the end game score (when one player gets 11 points). How can you fix it?
- How can you meet the game end condition without playing the game until 11, and without source modification?

CHAPTER 7

Debugging Asynchronous Operations

Debugging asynchronous JavaScript is fundamentally different and more complex than debugging synchronous code because the call stack no longer tells the whole story. In classic, synchronous JavaScript, you can step line by line, and the stack trace accurately reflects the path that led to the current state. Debugging sync code, you can be sure that nothing happened between the steps of the stack trace. With async code, the call stack is decoupled from the chronological flow. A breakpoint or a thrown exception can land you in an event loop task scheduled in another task, and god knows what happened between them.

In this chapter, you'll learn to make sense of this chaos by using developer tools and logging techniques. We'll start with the most important type of asynchronous operations for web applications: network requests.

Network Panel in Chrome Developer Tools

As soon as you open developer tools, the network panel starts recording all network requests, even while you're only using other panels. Let's take a closer look. Switch to the network panel in your developer tools (see the following image) and open the web page of the Pong game[1] we used in Chapter 6, Following the Data Flow, on page 77. You'll see something like the image at the top of the next page.

Read the Request List

Every line in the list is an HTTP request. The first one is the URL you have in the address bar, and it's usually an HTML document. As the browser downloads and parses the HTML, it takes every `<link>`, `<script>`, and `<img>`

1. https://oshibka404.github.io/pong/

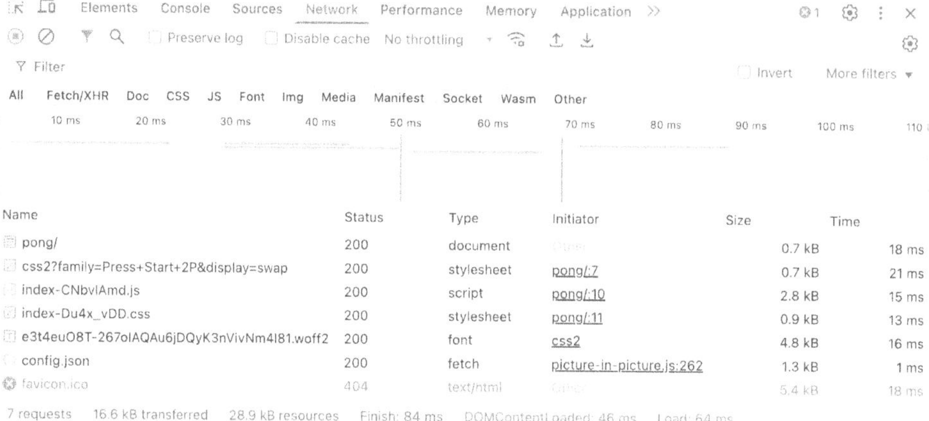

element it finds and makes an HTTP request to download the required resource: a CSS style sheet, a JavaScript file, or an image. The same goes for some <audio> and <video> elements, as well as fonts and image URLs linked in CSS files.

Next to each request, you'll see its status (200 for success), resource type, initiator, and time it took to complete the download, or it will have Memory Cache or Disk Cache in the Size column if the resource had been cached and the browser didn't have to download it again.

Requests that were not successful (with HTTP response codes other than 2xx or 3xx) will be written in red (see the favicon.ico request, for example).

Let's take a closer look at the Initiator column. Every cell contains a reference to the file and line where the request was triggered. Click the initiator of the JS request (pong/:10, line 10 of the document found by the pong/ path, as shown in the following image).

script pong/:10
stylesheet https://oshibka404.github.io/pong/

You'll find yourself on the familiar Sources tab, exactly on line 10 with the <script> element that triggered the request, as seen at the top of the next page.

Select any request by clicking it, and you'll see its details; you'll be able to inspect HTTP headers, request and response bodies, timings, cookies, and, on the Initiator tab, the call stack that triggered the request.

Some requests will be triggered not by the web page but by a browser extension. Then the protocol of the triggering file's URL will start from chrome-extension:, as seen in the next image.

Browser extensions not only trigger but also block requests. Typical examples are adblockers like uBlock and AdBlock Plus, and they can be a source of bugs that are hard to catch and reproduce. If your web shop fetches a price via an API call with a URL like analytics.myshop.com/get-price, you're likely to get some bug reports of the price not being displayed because a heuristic of some ad-blocking extension will misidentify it as a telemetry request. In general, you can't expect users to run only the extensions you want them to, and many will refuse to whitelist your site and compromise their privacy. While designing your APIs, be aware of the execution environment.

Just as common, requests can be blocked by a user's corporate firewall or be unavailable in certain countries or be on an ISP blacklist. The problem is so common that in many tech companies the questions "Do you have ad-blocking software installed?" and "Who is your internet service provider?" are a required step in the standard script of the first-line technical support.

So if you're investigating a bug and your hypothesis is a failed network request, how do you run an experiment to verify it? Yes, you can use a tool like Postman to mock the API endpoint or hard-code a failed response on the client side, but the easiest way is to block it on the browser level using developer tools.

Blocking Requests and Simulating Network Conditions

To simulate a failed HTTP request to a URL or a URL pattern, right-click a request in the list, and select Block Request URL:

This will open a Network Request Blocking panel below with the URL you selected added as an entry. Click the pencil icon on the right side and edit the blocking pattern. Use * for wildcard blocking. For example, use `*/search?q=*` to simulate a situation where all search queries fail:

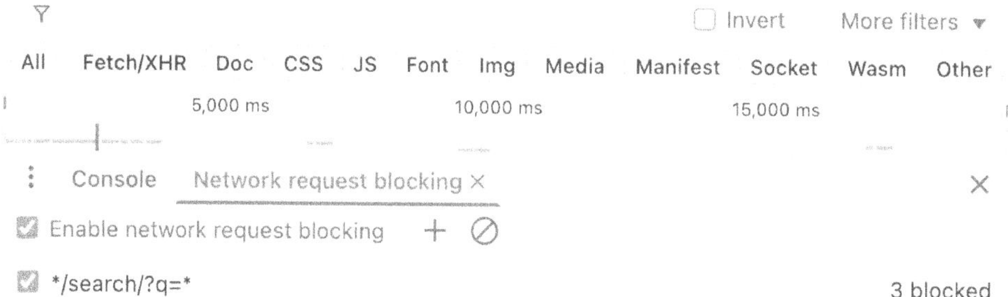

Another common cause of bugs in asynchronous code is slowness of requests rather than failure. This happens a lot when parts of the application assume that remotely fetched data are readily available or when timers and network requests are used together. You can simulate a poor and even broken connection using network throttling:

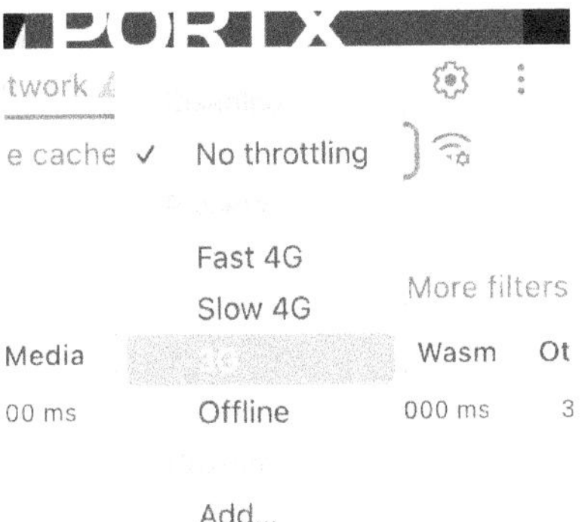

Even assuming the majority of your application's users live in places with stable internet connection (which is the case less often than people tend to think), you should proactively implement strategies to improve performance, such as optimizing images, leveraging caching, and minimizing HTTP requests. Simulating a slow connection helps you understand where to start.

Previewing Transitive Initiators

Hold down the Shift key and hover over a resource in the list. As shown in the following screenshot, it will highlight in red the resources that were requested from the hovered-over resource and highlight in green the resource that initiated the loading of the one you hover over.

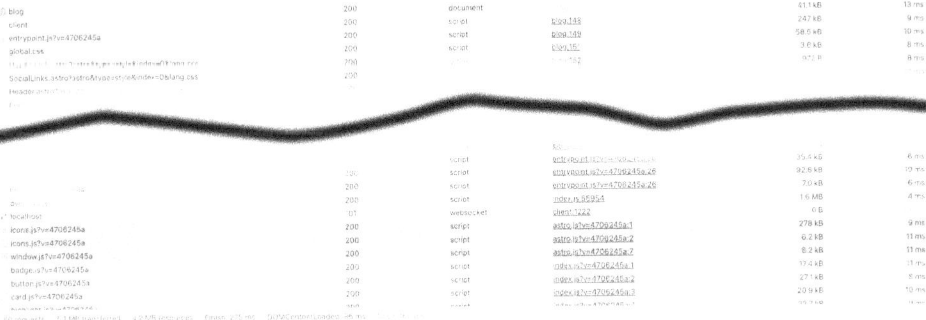

Note that it also highlights transitive initiators recursively, meaning that it highlights in green the resource that triggered the loading of the hovered-over resource, the resource that loaded that resource, and so on. The same goes for the other direction, but in red.

Filtering Requests

In the top bar, you can filter resources by type by clicking XHR, CSS, JS, and so on. You can select several types simultaneously by holding down the Command key.

Right above the resource type filters, you find the querying text field which supports regular expressions and a simple querying language allowing you to filter only resources of a certain size, from a certain domain, or of a certain content-type.

By adding a - before a word, you filter out resources matching the word. You can also use special property names. A basic autocompletion feature is even included, as the following image shows.

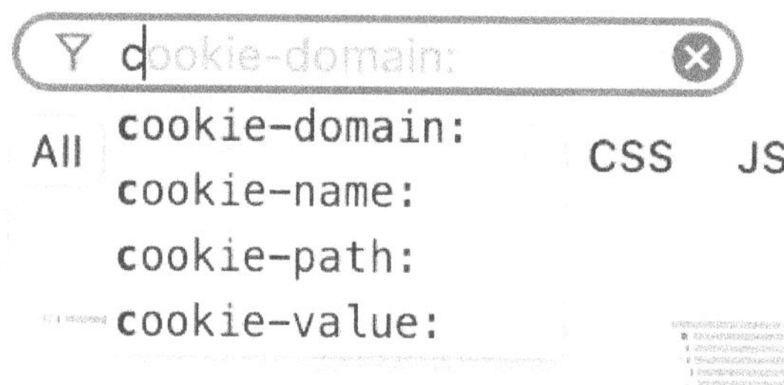

Combining the preceding techniques, the following image shows how you filter CSS and JS files larger than 100 KB and *not* having the word “astro” in their URLs:

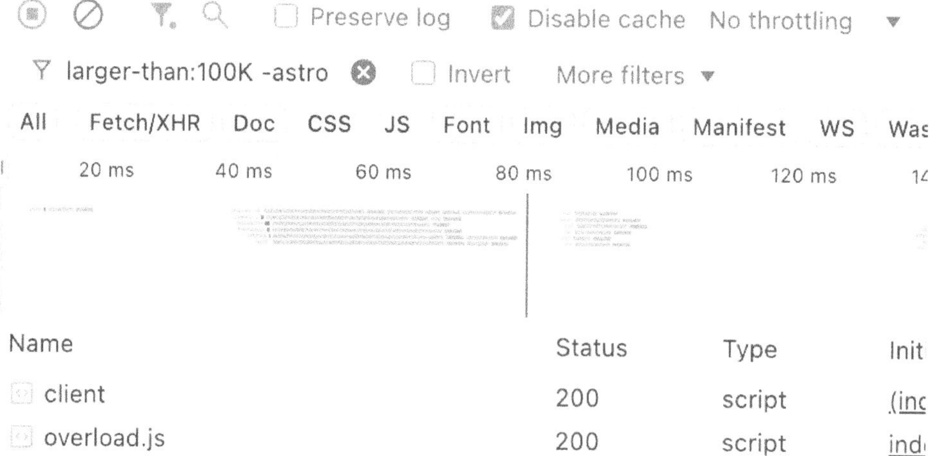

domain:framer.com, mime-type:application/json, method:put, and has-response-header:X-Frame-Options are all valid requests. You can refer to Chrome for developers[2] for the full list of query params.

The network panel shows only the requests that are filtered out by the current query. For example, type has-response-header:Cache-Control in the query field and enable the Invert Filter option, and you'll get only the resources that have no Cache-Control header.

Every query you type in can be applied in reverse by selecting the Invert Filter checkbox:

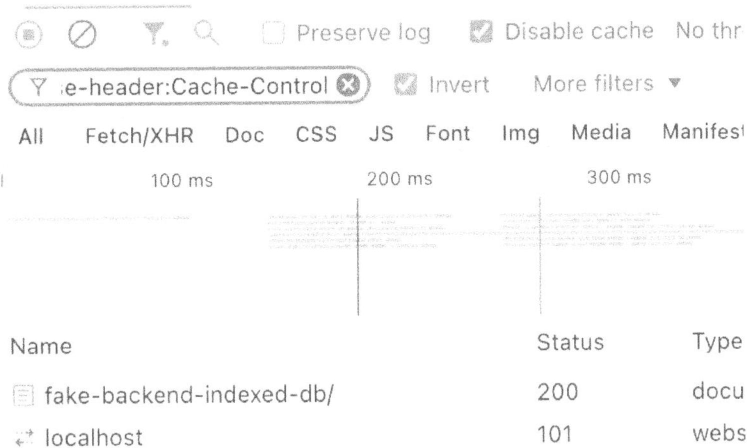

When you check it, the list shows only the resources that are blocked by extensions and by the Block Request URL we discussed earlier. It's useful to find that one little request is mistakenly blocked by an unknown office firewall and is breaking your app.

Use Full-Text Search

Full-text search is the button that I failed to notice for many years. As you can see in the following image, it's right there, between Filter and Preserve Log, both of which I used extensively.

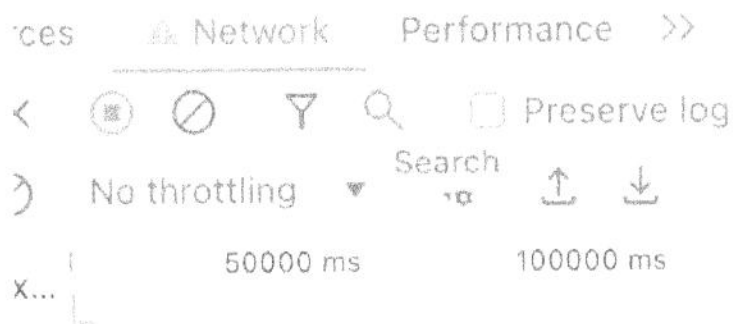

2. https://developer.chrome.com/docs/devtools/network/reference#filter-by-property

Type some text you see on the page into the search bar, hit Enter, and see all the network resources containing this text (see the next screenshot). Full-text search is useful for debugging a complex project where content comes from different APIs and modules are spread across repositories, and you want to know where to find the source.

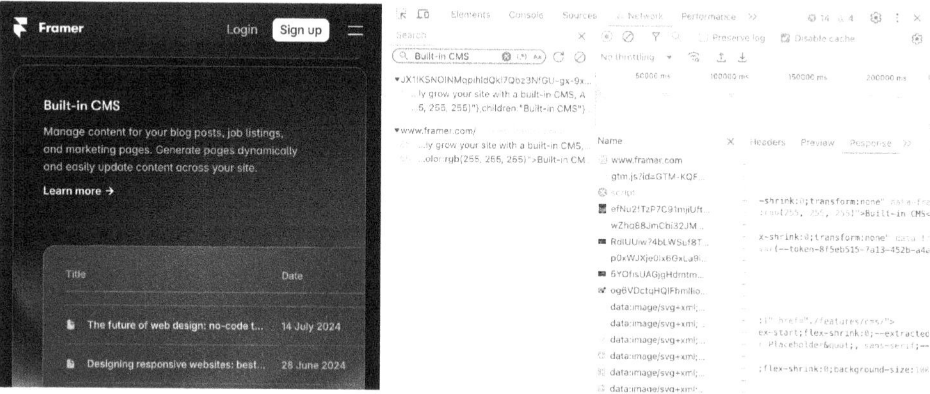

Apparently, in our case, it comes in both the HTML file contents and the JS file, which is a common pattern in server-side-generated pages: the full-page HTML is getting loaded and then "hydrated" with the JavaScript that's capable of generating exactly the same page to enable smooth SPA-style interactions. In a different case, we could just as well have found an XHR request or a static resource.

Search in HTTP Headers

Full-text search works not only across response bodies but across HTTP headers too. Also, it supports regular expressions and case-sensitive search (see the image at the top of the facing page). It's a handy thing.

‘ ### XHR Breakpoints

After you've carefully inspected network requests and figured out what can be causing bugs, you'll want to look more closely into the client code handling the request. One way to do this is by clicking the link in the Initiator tab of the network panel and setting a line breakpoint. However, it may not work out if the same code triggers many requests in your app, which is common when you have a network access layer. Also, you might miss some requests to the same URL triggered from other pieces of the code. A more reliable method is to set an XHR breakpoint.

In the Sources panel, in the same right sidebar where you find the call stack and the list of active breakpoints, expand XHR Breakpoints and press +. You

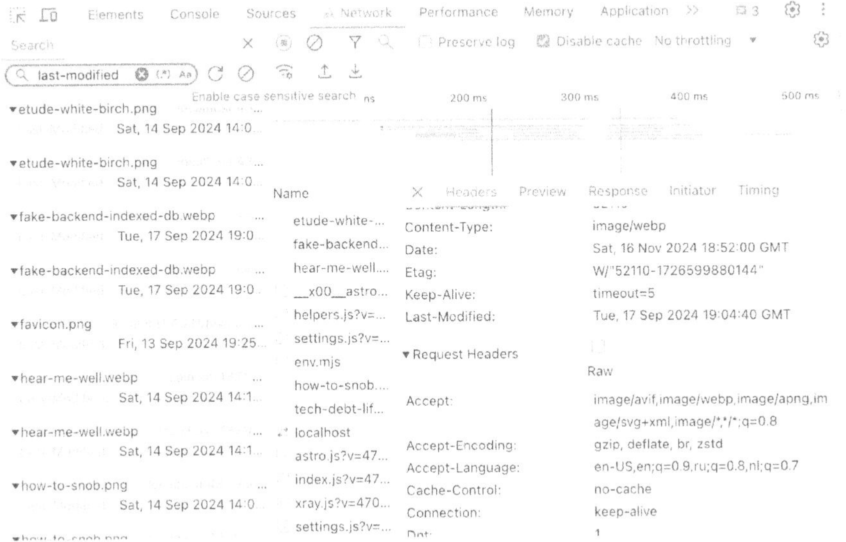

don't have to use * for wildcard in pattern; just type any part of the URL you want to pause on, or even leave it empty if you intend to pause execution on any XHR request:

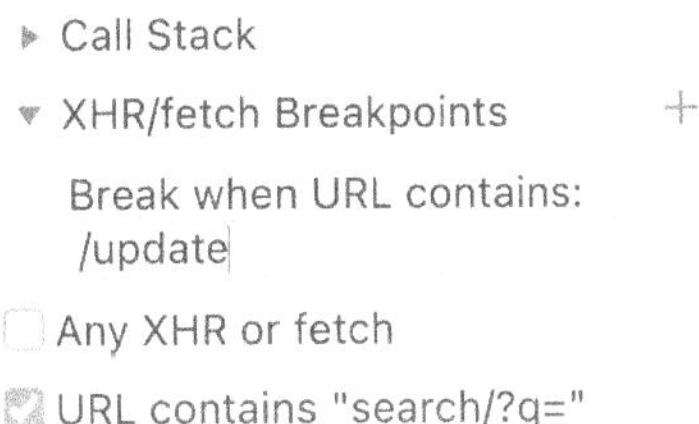

Now you can use the same techniques as in Chapter 6, Following the Data Flow, on page 77, and, going down the call stack, closely observe the code execution at every step.

Inspecting WebSocket Messages

Not all web network interactions follow the request-response pattern—take WebSockets, for instance. Press WS in the resource type filter. Click the request you're interested in and open the Messages subtab. Each row shows direction (color of the arrow), opcode, payload, and timestamp.

Click any row to expand long payloads or copy the raw frame. You can use the Initiator stack-trace link to jump to the JavaScript that opened the socket (see the image at the top of the next page).

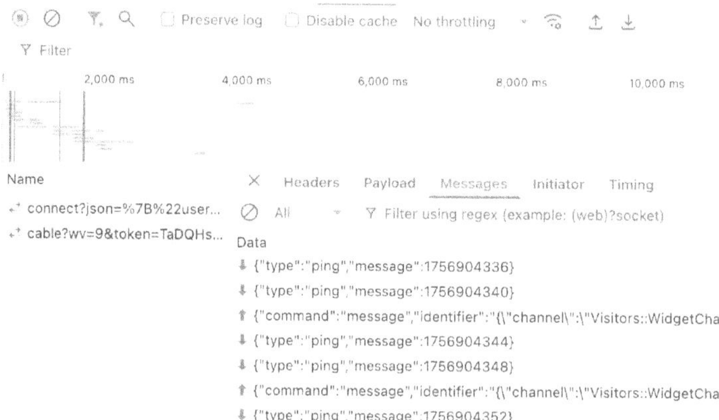

Debug Parallel Operations

Contrary to popular opinion, JavaScript has both concurrency and parallelism. Concurrency is all over the place wherever you see a `Promise`, an `async/await`, or even a `setTimeout` callback, but parallel operations are possible only with the explicit usage of workers or worklets. What's the difference between concurrency and parallelism?

Concurrency is the ability to make progress on more than one task during the same interval of time; JavaScript achieves it with a single-threaded event loop. Parallelism is true simultaneous execution on multiple CPU cores and is possible in JavaScript only with *workers*. Workers spawn separate OS-level threads that run in parallel to the main thread, and they exchange data via messages.

Without workers, JavaScript is strictly single-threaded, and its many operations—timers, network requests, user input—are handled concurrently without parallelism.

Debugging Workers and Audio Worklets

Practically speaking, there's not much difference between debugging parallel code (workers, worklets) and event loop-based asynchronous code. Modern browsers list source files of workers and worklets under the Sources tab in exactly the same way as the main thread files. One meaningful difference is that you lose parts of the call stack that precede the spawning of the thread. The other is that while the execution of a worker thread is stopped, the event loop in the main thread keeps running, which makes interactive debugging of cross-thread applications more complicated.

Code executed in an <iframe> may or may not be executed in a separate thread, depending on the domain of the iframe and the browser. Generally, frames on the same origin share the system process and those on different domains don't, but it's not a strictly defined behavior, so you shouldn't rely on it.

You can use a header called Origin-Agent-Cluster to explicitly ask the browser to spawn a separate thread for the scripts running on this origin (and you can read it in Window.originAgentCluster). At the time of writing this paragraph, this header is supported by all major browsers except Safari, but even the browsers supporting it are not required to honor the request. So the only way to reliably write a multithreaded JavaScript code is using workers.

A lightweight version of workers, called worklets, also exists. They're used to provide low-latency interfaces to audio and video rendering and, when possible, are executed on the audio or video card chip. Debugging them can get hard because of their real-time nature. They're supposed to be called multiple times per second, computing screen frame images or sound samples, with the results of the previous calls affecting the next one.

This is one of the reasons why, while debugging parallel code, logging is often more convenient than interactive debugging with breakpoints; logging is nondisruptive. You can use console both from workers and in the browser console.

Let's implement an audio worklet that takes input from the microphone, repeats it to the audio output, and reports to the main thread every time it does so. The global currentTime variable we're using is a read-only property available in audio worklets and stores a floating-point number representing the time.

```
class LogProcessor extends AudioWorkletProcessor {
  constructor() {
    super()
    console.debug('LogProcessor initialized')
  }

  process(inputs, outputs, parameters) {
    // Send a log message every 128 frames (standard block size)
    console.debug(`Processing block at ${currentTime.toFixed(3)}s`),
    })
    return true // Keep processor alive
  }
}

registerProcessor('log-processor', LogProcessor)
```

It works, but problems arise as soon as you want to use logging techniques other than console. You cannot print a log message on a page, because a worker's thread does not have access to DOM. You can send HTTP requests directly from WebWorkers (not from worklets) using fetch, but once you want to send them through the same layers as the main thread does, fetch becomes insufficient. You need to first send logs to the main thread, and the only way to do that is by using MessagePort. We'll have to put in some effort to make better logging possible.

```
class LogProcessor extends AudioWorkletProcessor {
  constructor() {
    super()
    this.port.postMessage({ type: 'log', message: 'LogProcessor initialized' })
  }

  process(inputs, outputs, parameters) {
    // Send a log message every 128 frames (standard block size)
    this.port.postMessage({
      type: 'log',
      message: `Processing block at ${currentTime.toFixed(3)}s`,
    })
    return true // Keep processor alive
  }
}

registerProcessor('log-processor', LogProcessor);
```

To use the message received from the audio worklet in the main thread, we'll check if the received message has the "log" type and, if it does, we'll print the message. We need to check the message type because in most real scenarios you'll need other message types as well, like control messages (start, stop, pause, and so on).

```
const audioContext = new AudioContext()
await audioContext.audioWorklet.addModule('log-processor.js')

const logNode = new AudioWorkletNode(audioContext, 'log-processor')
logNode.connect(audioContext.destination)

logNode.port.onmessage = (event) => {
  if (event.data.type === 'log') {
    // here comes the logging technique we prefer to use
    console.log(event.data.message)
  }
}

logNode.port.start()
```

Every time this worklet processes a block of audio data, it will send a message using postMessage to the main thread, and it will be printed to the browser console.

Logging on a Web Page

As we've seen with workers, logging becomes essential while debugging asynchronous operations when relative timing of concurrent operations matters. We discussed logging using the browser console in Chapter 1, Printing and Interpreting Errors, on page 1, and we'll talk about collecting logs in Chapter 8, Make Your Code Debuggable, on page 113.

In addition to console and collected logs, you might want to log debug info right on the page during development but, of course, not in production. Let's achieve it by using the environment variables we used in Chapter 5, Designing Software That Doesn't Break, on page 53. First, let's append a debug area when in the development environment:

```
// debug-logger.js
let debugNode
if (import.meta.env.DEV) {
    debugNode = document.createElement('pre')
    debugNode.id = 'debug-node'
    document.body.appendChild(debugNode)
}
```

Let's position it on the page as an overlay:

```
#debug-node {
    position: fixed;
    top: 0;
    right: 0;
    max-height: 100%;
    font-family: monospace;
    width: 25%;
    background-color: rgba(255, 255, 255, .1);
}
```

Now, in the same logger.js file, do this:

```
// logger.js
export function debugLog(message) {
    const debugNode = document.getElementById('debug-node')

    if (debugNode) {
        debugNode.textContent += message + '\n'
    }
}
```

Wrapping Up

In this chapter, you learned to read and navigate HTTP requests and WebSocket messages. You learned to inspect their headers, timings, and bodies, as well as visualize what triggered them and debug related client code. You learned the difference between concurrent and parallel code and how to debug code in other threads using inter-thread messages and logging.

In the next chapter, we'll step beyond logging and discuss debuggability at large. We'll talk about not only how we print and read logs but also how we store and analyze them and how we send alerts when things go seriously wrong.

CHAPTER 8

Make Your Code Debuggable

We've already covered many essential debugging techniques to help you deal with the bugs you've found. We discussed bug reproduction, interactive breakpoint-based debugging, logging, and reporting. We talked about bug management and the principles of bug-free software design to deal with software quality on a system level. The next step is to learn to build debuggable systems.

Debuggability is how easily a system allows developers to diagnose and locate defects. A debuggable system provides contextualized and actionable information, exposing not just what went wrong but why and where it happened. Having all the errors, logs, and traces consolidated and systematized helps enormously.

In this chapter, we'll be using Sentry because it's simple to set up, easily scalable, and has a generous free plan and a big online community. We'll start by monitoring JavaScript errors, then add structured logs and enrich them with metadata. You'll also learn to query both errors and logs, but first let's set up Sentry.

Setting Up Sentry

You'll need a Sentry account. After you sign up,[1] create a project for the front end (see the following image). When part of your web application runs on a server, you'll set up a separate project for the back end, and when your back end consists of multiple services, you'll set up a project per service. It's the same if your front-end code is split between multiple repos, but you might want to create a project per logical part. Don't worry about losing the full picture—Sentry supports distributed traces and will show you the chain of events having happened across multiple projects as a single linear story.

1. https://sentry.io/signup/

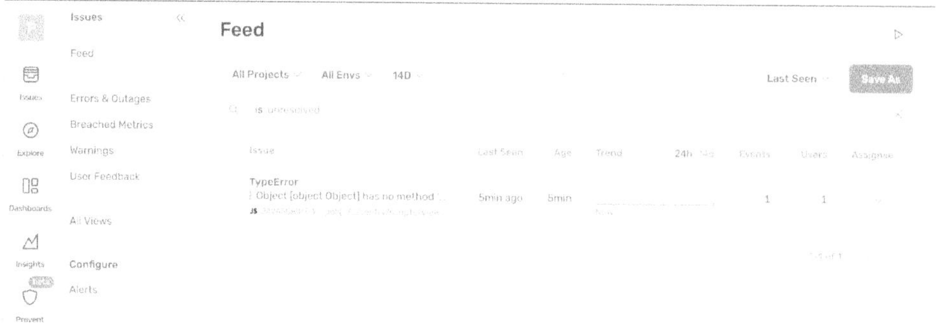

To set up the SDK, you'll need the DSN key for the project. Find it in Project Settings > SDK Setup > Client Keys (DSN) (see the image that follows). We'll need it in the next step.

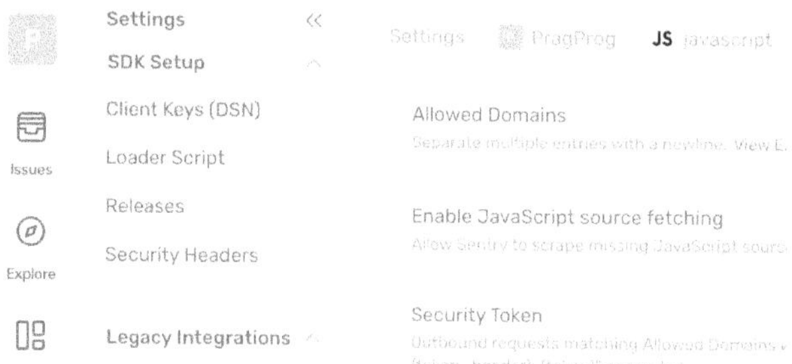

After you've created a project and found your DSN key, we'll run the application we'll be monitoring and set up Sentry SDK.

Run a Sample Application

You can follow this chapter using your own source code; all the steps should apply with minimal adjustments. However, I'll be explaining them using a sample React application, available from GitHub,[2] so to follow the steps exactly one-to-one, fork the project and clone it onto your local machine:

```
git clone git@github.com:<your_username>/frontend-tutorial.git
```

Let's run the application:

```
yarn # install dependencies
yarn start # run the application
```

Open it in the browser, http://localhost:3000 (shown at the top of the next page).

2. https://github.com/oshibka404/frontend-tutorial

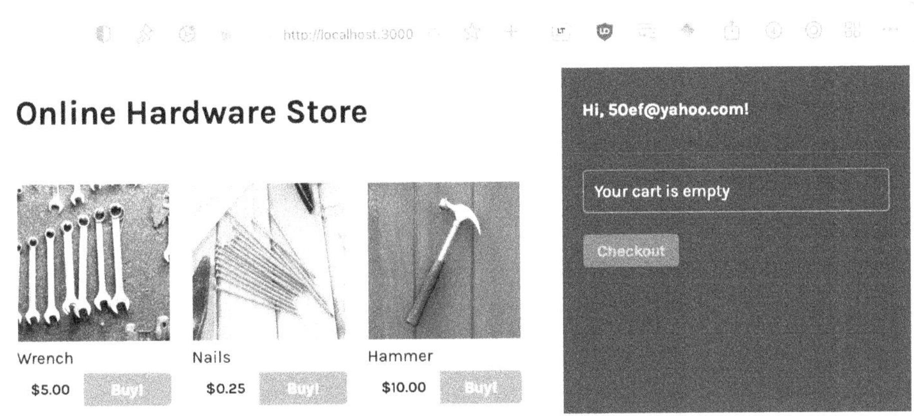

Initialize the SDK

We're running a React application, so we'll use React SDK. Run the following terminal command from the root of the project:

```
yarn add @sentry/react
```

You'll see separate specialized SDKs for many other frameworks and a general-purpose JavaScript SDK.

Open the src/index.js file and initialize Sentry SDK by importing it and calling init on it:

```
import * as Sentry from "@sentry/react";

Sentry.init({
  dsn: "<your_DSN_key>", // paste the DSN key from profile setings
}
```

From now on, Sentry SDK will be capturing and logging exceptions thrown by your application's runtime. Note that it will capture only the exceptions caught after the initialization, so try to initialize the SDK as early as possible in your application's life cycle.

Monitoring Errors

To see error monitoring working, you need errors. Let's add one. If you're following this chapter using your own source code, then I assume by now you know a dozen ways, so use any of them. Otherwise, uncomment line 97 in src/components/App.js:

```
this.myCodeIsPerfect();
```

The method myCodeIsPerfect() isn't defined, so this call is supposed to throw a TypeError, once executed.

Save the file, refresh your browser, and open the browser console. The error we've introduced is in the checkout method. Click any of the Buy! buttons to add products to your shopping cart. Click the Checkout button on the right panel to generate an error (shown in the following image).

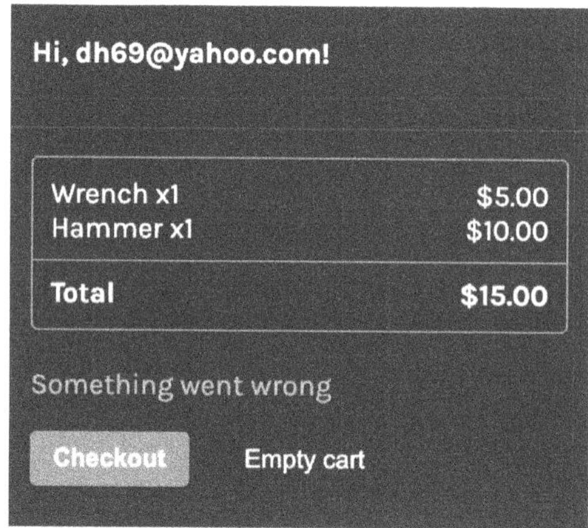

After this, three things should happen: an error message, Something Went Wrong, displays in the app; the error with a stack trace appears in the browser console, and you receive an email alert about the error (see the following two images).

```
Uncaught TypeError: this.myCodeIsMorePerfect is not a function
    at App.checkout (App.js:97:10)
  Show ignore-listed frames
```

Give the email (shown on the next page) a couple of minutes to arrive. Open the issue by clicking a link in the email, or navigate to the issues feed from your Sentry Dashboard and click the latest one.

Notice how many details are captured there: browser version, operating system, IP address, URL, and, if you scroll the page down, the full readable stack trace of the erroneous call.

Unfortunately, the stack trace is nice and readable only because we were running our app in development mode, where JavaScript minification is skipped. Let's see what it looks like when the code is minified, like it normally is in production builds.

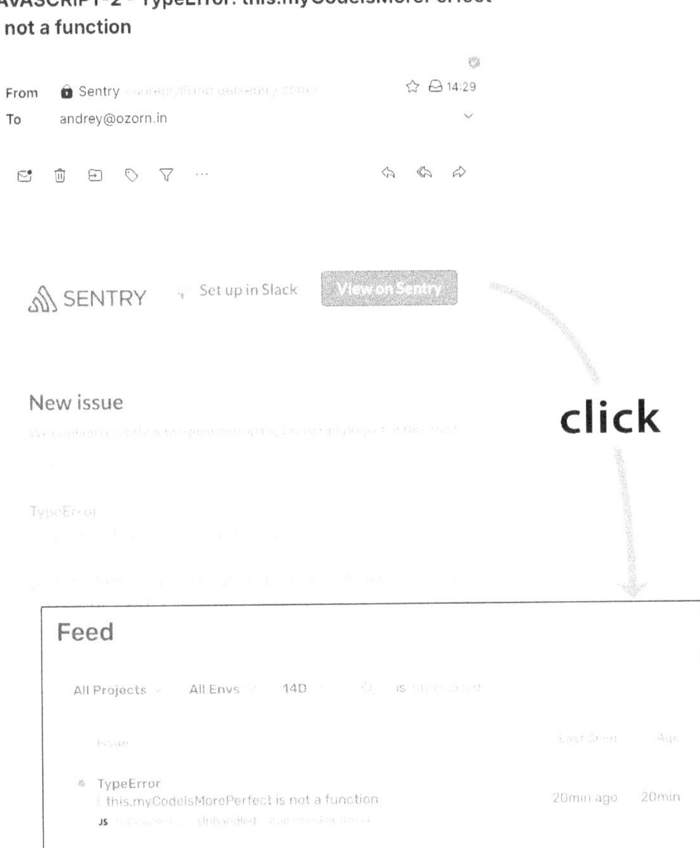

Stop the development server by pressing Control+C in the terminal and then type the following:

```
yarn build
npx serve build
```

This will run the application build in production mode and serve the built files at localhost:3000. Repeat the error reproduction steps (add items to cart and press Checkout), and you'll have a different issue reported to Sentry. When you open it, you'll see that the stack trace isn't that helpful anymore and mostly contains items with names like Object.Ae, $e, and t.value, as shown at the top of the next page

Now, let's make the stack traces readable again.

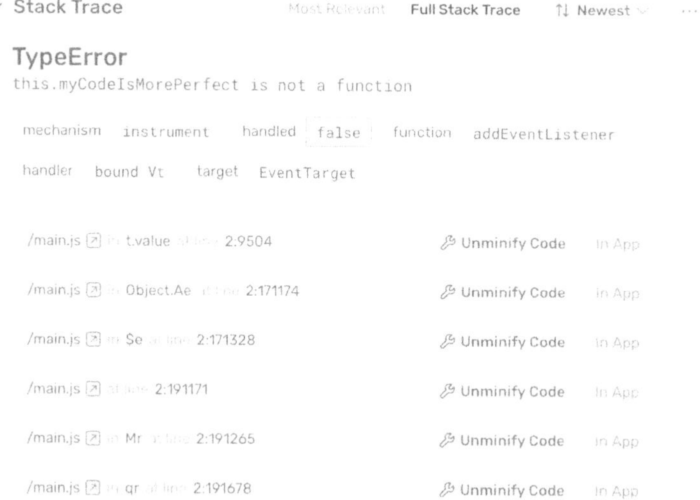

Enable Readable Stack Traces

Remember, in Chapter 6, Following the Data Flow, on page 77, we covered how to set up source maps? We'll now use this knowledge to generate and upload them to Sentry.

First, we need the source maps. Our demo project uses webpack, whose configuration file is found in webpack.config.js. Open the file and uncomment line 11, and save the file:

```
devtool: "source-map",
```

Now run the production build:

```
yarn build
```

In the root of the demo project, you should find a new folder build. Inside, there should be a main.js file and a main.js.map file. main.js is the minified JavaScript, and main.js.map is the source map file. Upload it using Sentry's webpack plugin:

```
yarn add @sentry/webpack-plugin --dev
npx @sentry/wizard@latest -i sourcemaps
```

If you're following this chapter with your own source code, and it's using vite as we did in previous chapters, follow the same steps, but using the Vite plugin instead:

```
yarn add @sentry/vite-plugin --dev
```

Next, you'll need an authorization token, which you generate in the Sentry web interface by opening Settings > Developer Settings > Organization Tokens and pressing Create New Token (see the following image).

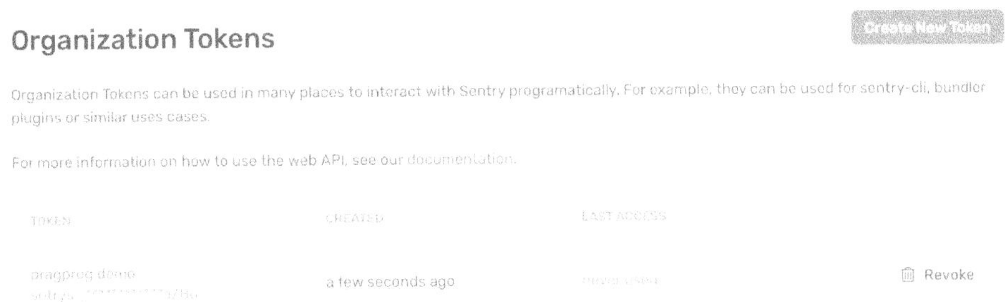

Never commit your auth tokens, ever. Once you accidentally commit them, consider them compromised forever—revoke them and generate new ones.

The right way to store your authorization tokens is in environment variables, and then use them the same way we accessed NODE_ENV in Chapter 5, Designing Software That Doesn't Break, on page 53, via process.env.

Run this in your terminal:

```
export SENTRY_AUTH_TOKEN=<Your_token>
```

If you're following using your own source code and are going to need the token later, add the export to .zshrc (or .bashrc, depending on the shell you're using).

Configure the Sentry plugin in the webpack.config.js file:

```
plugins: [
    sentryWebpackPlugin({
       org: "<Your_org>",
       project: "<Your_project>",
       authToken: process.env.SENTRY_AUTH_TOKEN,
    }),
 ],
```

You can find your org as part of your Sentry URL (for example, https://YOUR_ORG.sentry.io).

Run yarn build again and read the logs. They should contain something like this:

```
[sentry-webpack-plugin]
Info: Sending telemetry data on issues and performance to Sentry.
To disable telemetry, set `options.telemetry` to `false`.
...
[sentry-webpack-plugin] Info: Successfully uploaded source maps to Sentry
```

Run npx serve build again to serve the production build, open the app at localhost:3000, and trigger the error again.

Go to the Issues page in Sentry. Since you added a new release, a new issue should be created even though it's the same error as before. Click the new issue to open its Issue Details page:

Stack Trace   Most Relevant   Full Stack Trace   Newest

TypeError
this.myCodeIsMorePerfect is not a function

mechanism instrument handled false function addEventListener
handler bound Wt target EventTarget

frontend-tutorial-2/./src/components/App.js in r.value at line 97:10   In App

```
    // });
  }

  checkout() {
    // Generate an error
    this.myCodeIsMorePerfect();

```

Notice that the stack trace is not only readable now but also allows you to browse code around each item of the stack trace.

Scroll the page to see how much more context you have now: build number; breadcrumbs, including the release tag; sequence of clicks in UI, and console errors preceding the reported issue (shown at the top of the facing page). Most of the time, you don't need anything else to reproduce the issue and start investigating it from the right place.

However, you can take one more step to significantly narrow down the search field for the root-cause analysis—enable stack trace linking and suspect commits.

Enable Stack Trace Linking

Sentry can use commit metadata from your source code repositories to suggest suspect commits that might have introduced an error. You can find them right on your Issue Details page. Commit tracking is especially useful when multiple people are working on a project because it lets Sentry display suggested assignees—the list of the authors of those suspect commits. Before we can enable commit tracking, we'll first need to set up GitHub integration and give Sentry access to the repository.

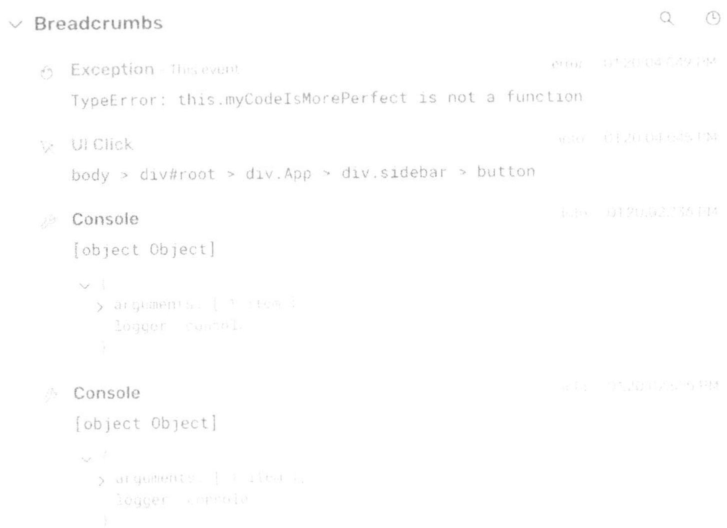

In Sentry, go to Settings > Integrations > GitHub and press Add Installation:

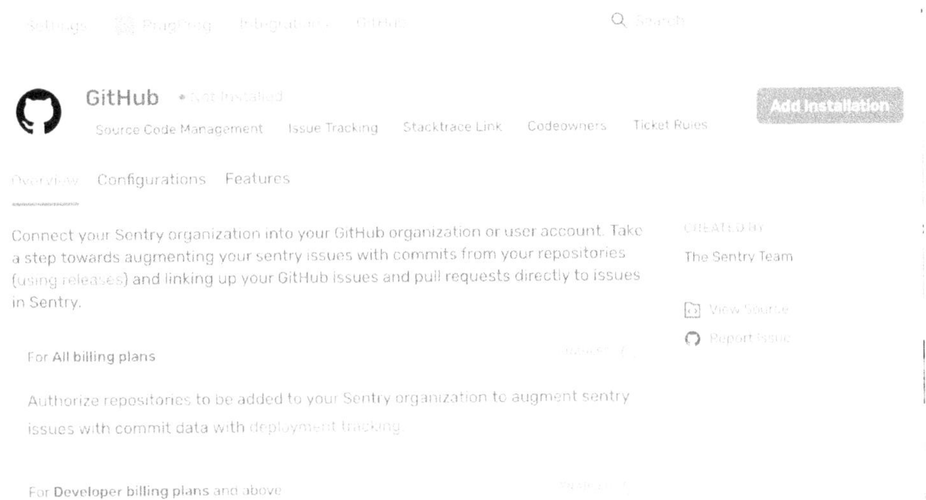

Select the repositories Sentry should have access to. You should then be redirected back to Sentry Integrations and see the list of repositories you authorized.

Go to the Code Mappings tab and click Add Code Mapping. Select the repository where your application lives and specify the source code directory (in our case, src), as shown in the next image.

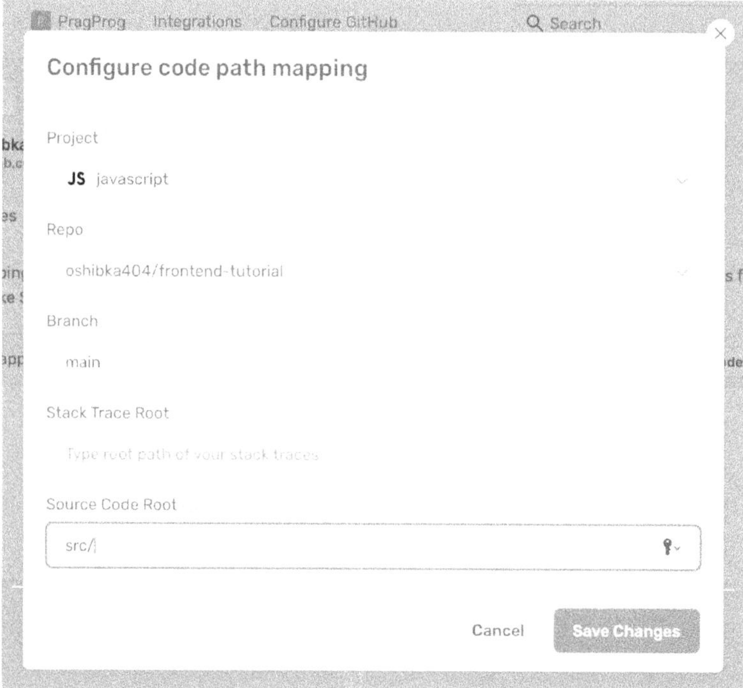

At this point, when you open the latest issue, you'll see a button Open This Line in GitHub:

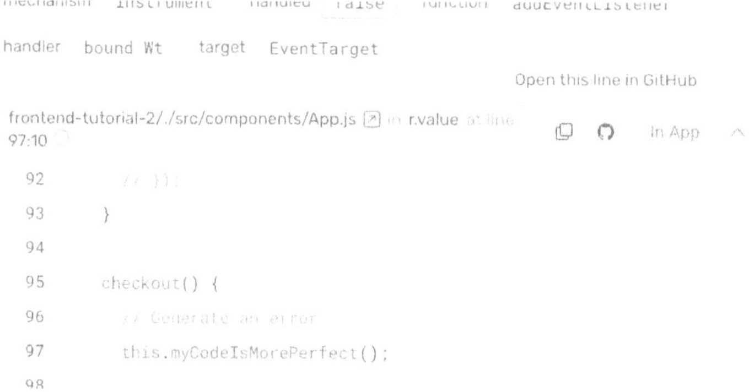

We've set up code mapping that matches the stack trace entries with the source files on GitHub. It will point to the lines of code, but won't yet immediately point to the suspect commit. Knowing the commit would be handy. Let's set it up.

Enable Suspect Commits

We've already created and exported the SENTRY_AUTH_TOKEN. Check if it's still available in your terminal:

```
echo $SENTRY_AUTH_TOKEN
```

If it's not available, repeat the steps from the previous section where we generated the authorization token.

To start associating commits and releases, add the release field to your Sentry webpack plugin config in webpack.config.js:

```
sentryWebpackPlugin({
  org: "<Your_org>",
  project: "<Your_project>",
  authToken: process.env.SENTRY_AUTH_TOKEN,

  release: {
    create: true,
    setCommits: {
       auto: true,
    },
  },
}),
```

Edit the line in src/App.tsx where we previously triggered errors by calling this.myCodeIsPerfect(). Change it to any other nonexistent name, so that Sentry recognizes it as a different issue.

```
this.myCodeIsMorePerfect()
```

Commit the change:

```
git commit -am 'Added a new error'
git push
```

Now, after you run another production build, the webpack plugin will create a new release and associate your commit to that release.

```
yarn build
```

Start the webpack server:

```
npx serve build
```

Reproduce the error: open localhost:3000, add items to cart, and check out. The new issue description will have the suspect commit in both an email alert and a web application (see the following image).

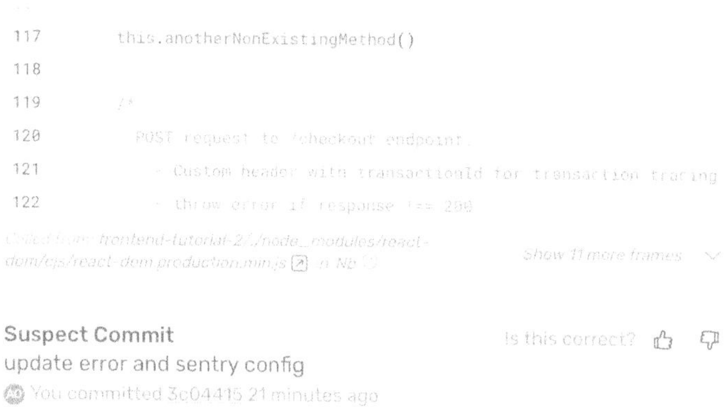

```
this.anotherNonExistingMethod()

/*
  POST request to /checkout endpoint.
    - Custom header with transactionId for transaction tracing
    - throw error if response != 200
```

frontend-tutorial-2/./node_modules/react-dom/cjs/react-dom.production.min.js in Nb

Show 11 more frames

Suspect Commit

update error and sentry config

You committed 3c04415 21 minutes ago

Is this correct?

At this point, we have every issued error reported to a centralized place—Sentry. Similar issues are grouped together and have stats on which platforms, browsers, and operating systems they were encountered, what user actions preceded the errors, and on which release versions they happened. In addition, we have suspect commits suggested and have a direct link to source files of the stack trace items on GitHub. All this together will simplify any future investigation enormously by immediately providing valuable context to every issue. Let's add even more details to the context and, beside reported errors, add structured logs.

Structured Logs

Structured logs allow you to send, view, and query text-based log messages in Sentry. Once in Sentry, these logs can be viewed alongside relevant errors and searched by text-string or by using their individual attributes.

Let's set it up. Open `index.js` and edit SDK initialization by adding the `enableLogs` option set to `true`:

```
Sentry.init({
  dsn: "<your_dsn>",
  enableLogs: true,
});
```

Enabling this feature on the SDK allows you to send logs using the `Sentry.logger` namespace.

Similar to the Console API we discussed in Chapter 1, Printing and Interpreting Errors, on page 1, the `Sentry.logger` namespace exposes six methods that you can use to log messages at different log levels: `trace`, `debug`, `info`, `warn`, `error`, and `fatal`. Of those six, only `fatal` is not present in Console API.

As a second argument to all of these methods, you're allowed to pass a free-form object, and that is where these logs become truly structured. You'll be able to query by the values of this object.

```
Sentry.logger.warn("Rate limit reached for endpoint", {
  endpoint: "/api/results/",
  isEnterprise: false,
});
```

Console Logging Integration

You can configure the SDK to intercept all the calls to the browser's console logging API and send these logs to Sentry. It's especially nice if you already have many console log calls in the code and you want to reuse them as structured logs and store them in a centralized location. To set it up, add Sentry.consoleLoggingIntegration to the integrations array of the SDK initialization in index.js.

```
Sentry.init({
  dsn: "<Your_DSN>",
  integrations: [
      // send console.log, console.warn, and console.error calls as logs
      // to Sentry
      Sentry.consoleLoggingIntegration({ levels: ["log", "warn", "error"] }),
  ],
  enableLogs: true,
});
```

The consoleLoggingIntegration accepts a levels option, which is an array of console method names to log. By default, the integration will log calls from console.debug, console.info, console.warn, console.error, console.log, console.assert, and console.trace.

If you provide multiple arguments to your console object calls, the integration will parse them as different attributes, which can be searched and filtered for in the Sentry UI.

```
console.log("Executed Action for User:", 123, true);
```

Filtering Logs

Too many logs can be noisy, so you might want to send only a subset of them by filtering the ones you consider useless. Let's add the beforeSendLog option to the same initialization call in index.js.

```
beforeSendLog: (log) => {
  if (log.level === "info") {
    // Filter out all info logs
    return null;
  }
```

```
  if (log.attributes.environment === "development") {
    // Don't send logs from debugging environment
    return null;
  }

  // enrich logs with metadata in attributes
  log.attributes.timeSinceLastUpdate = Date.now() - getLastUpdateTime()

  return log;
},
```

Using beforeSendLog, we won't be sending logs from the app running in the development environment, because it's normal to have an app break during development, and sending every log would cause false alarms. We also add an attribute timeSinceLastUpdate. It can be any attribute with any JSON-serializable value. You'll be able to query logs using their values.

The JavaScript SDK will automatically add some attributes for you, including environment (for example, development or production, same as process.env.NODE_ENV), release (the release ID set in the SDK, if defined), sdk.name—the name of the SDK that sent the log ("javascript" in our case), and sdk.version (the version of the SDK that sent the log).

You can find and explore logs in Sentry by going to Explore > Logs.

Above the graph, you'll find filters to query the logs by message text, severity level, and any other attributes, including the ones we've added. As an example of a custom attribute we added in the beforeSendLog function, try typing its name, timeSinceLastUpdate, in the search field. Then type in "total" and play around with the value. This is shown in the image at the top of the facing page.

In a similar way to logs, you can explore issues, filtering them by text, date, severity, and all other attributes, both standard and custom.

Adding Performance Traces

With tracing, Sentry automatically tracks your software performance across your application services, measuring metrics like throughput and latency, and displaying the impact of errors across multiple systems.

By default, every transaction will be sent to Sentry. It's good for testing, but once testing is complete, you should define a lower sample rate by setting the tracesSampleRate value in the init config. If you leave your sample rate at 1.0, a transaction will be sent every time a user loads a page or navigates within your app. Depending on the amount of traffic your application gets, this may mean a lot of transactions.

Once Sentry.browserTracingIntegration is added to the SDK configuration, the Sentry SDK starts to immediately create a new transaction for each page load and navigation event and a child span for every XMLHttpRequest or fetch request that occurs while those transactions are open.

Sentry Tracing Concepts

- A trace is a record of a series of connected events and operations coming from your application. Each trace is composed of spans.
- A span is a named, timed operation that represents a part of the application workflow, like fetch requests, long computations, or database queries. Spans have attributes and metrics.
- Span attributes and metrics are pieces of information captured for each span. Attributes are key-value pairs providing additional context (for example, the name of the operation). Metrics are numerical values measuring the performance of the span (for example, the duration of the operation).
- A transaction is a unit that represents any event that your application sends to Sentry, like loading a web page or processing an API call. A transaction contains one or more spans.

Explore Traces

On Sentry, open Explore > Traces, and select a metric to observe (for example, span.duration for the time between requests). Change the grouping and sorting on the left, and change the filter query on the top. You'll visualize the performance rate of your application (see the following image).

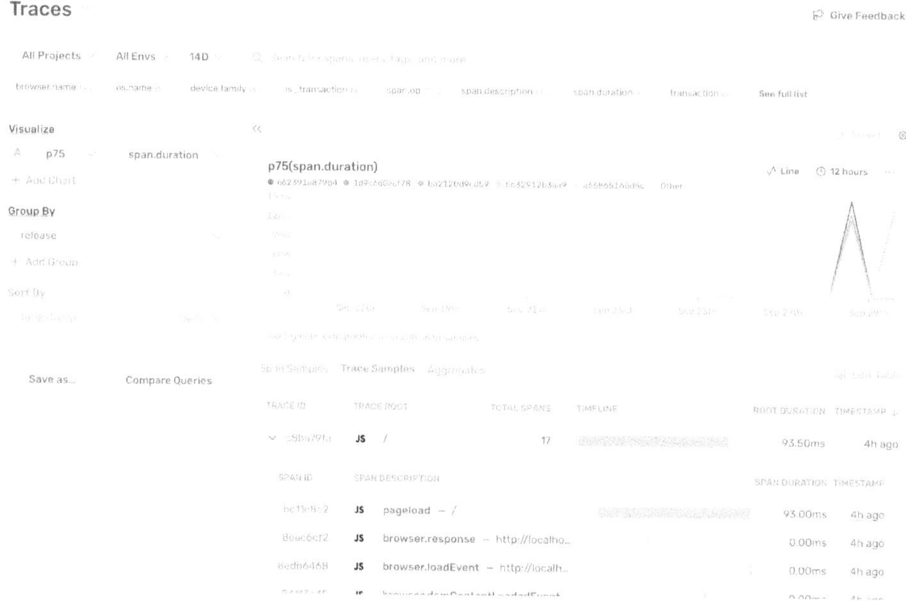

Add Custom Traces

You can also manually start spans to instrument specific parts of your code. This is useful when you want to measure the performance of a specific operation or function.

Spans are especially helpful with contextual attributes. Aside from performance metrics, you can add business metrics.

```
// Adding business context to a payment processing span
Sentry.startSpan(
  {
    name: "Process Payment",
    op: "payment.process",
    attributes: {
      "payment.amount": 99.99,
      "payment.currency": "USD",
      "payment.method": "credit_card",
      "customer.type": "returning",
    },
  },
```

```
  async () => {
    // Payment processing implementation
  },
);
```

Logs, traces, and metrics are the three pillars of observability, and their consolidation in one tool lets you have a single telemetry pipeline. Using a single pipeline requires much less maintenance than managing multiple systems.

Wrapping Up

We've reached the end of the book. I hope it's been as exciting a reading journey for you as it was an incredible writing journey for me. Starting at logging and throwing errors, we went through reliable software design to bug reproduction and prioritization. We took a closer look at some parts of Chrome developer tools and finished by building front-end debuggability using Sentry.

Debuggability is easier to get right when you have a feel for what debugging looks like, what the typical error paths are, and what information you'll be missing when things go wrong. You can get knowledge and understanding from books and articles, but you'll only develop real mastery from active, repeated debugging sessions. Keep learning, and practice, practice, practice.

Thank you!

We hope you enjoyed this book and that you're already thinking about what you want to learn next. To help make that decision easier, we're offering you this gift.

Head on over to https://pragprog.com right now, and use the coupon code BUYANOTHER2026 to save 30% on your next ebook. Offer is void where prohibited or restricted. This offer does not apply to any edition of *The Pragmatic Programmer* ebook.

And if you'd like to share your own expertise with the world, why not propose a writing idea to us? After all, many of our best authors started off as our readers, just like you. With up to a 50% royalty, world-class editorial services, and a name you trust, there's nothing to lose. Visit https://pragprog.com/become-an-author/ today to learn more and to get started.

Thank you for your continued support. We hope to hear from you again soon!

The Pragmatic Bookshelf

Modern CSS with Tailwind, Second Edition

Tailwind CSS is an exciting new CSS framework that allows you to design your site by composing simple utility classes to create complex effects. With Tailwind, you can style your text, move your items on the page, design complex page layouts, and adapt your design for devices from a phone to a wide-screen monitor. With this book, you'll learn how to use Tailwind for its flexibility and its consistency, from the smallest detail of your typography to the entire design of your site.

Noel Rappin
(102 pages) ISBN: 9781680509403. $29.95
https://pragprog.com/book/tailwind2

Vector Search with JavaScript

Make search results smarter and more useful for everyday users and deliver more relevant results with vector search. Go beyond keyword matching to build search experiences that understand meaning, context, and similarity. Use AI-powered techniques to create recommendation systems, personalized search, and content discovery tools. Implement vector search from the ground up with step-by-step guidance, real-world examples, and hands-on coding. Generate embeddings, construct vector indexes, and optimize search accuracy with practical methods that integrate seamlessly into JavaScript applications. Whether refining an existing project or developing a new one, unlock the power of AI-driven search to create smarter, more intuitive user experiences.

Ben Greenberg
(128 pages) ISBN: 9798888651735. $35.95
https://pragprog.com/book/bgvector

Test-Driving JavaScript Applications

Debunk the myth that JavaScript is not easily testable. Whether you use Node.js, Express, MongoDB, jQuery, AngularJS, or directly manipulate the DOM, you can test-drive JavaScript. Learn the craft of writing meaningful, deterministic automated tests with Karma, Mocha, and Chai. Test asynchronous JavaScript, decouple and properly mock out dependencies, measure code coverage, and create lightweight modular designs of both server-side and client-side code. Your investment in writing tests will pay high dividends as you create code that's predictable and cost-effective to change.

Venkat Subramaniam
(362 pages) ISBN: 9781680501742. $38
https://pragprog.com/book/vsjavas

A Common-Sense Guide to Data Structures and Algorithms in JavaScript, Volume 1

If you thought data structures and algorithms were all just theory, you're missing out on what they can do for your JavaScript code. Learn to use Big O notation to make your code run faster by orders of magnitude. Choose from data structures such as hash tables, trees, and graphs to increase your code's efficiency exponentially. With simple language and clear diagrams, this book makes this complex topic accessible, no matter your background. Every chapter features practice exercises to give you the hands-on information you need to master data structures and algorithms for your day-to-day work.

Jay Wengrow
(514 pages) ISBN: 9798888650646. $69.95
https://pragprog.com/book/jwjavascript

The Pragmatic Bookshelf

The Pragmatic Bookshelf features books written by professional developers for professional developers. The titles continue the well-known Pragmatic Programmer style and continue to garner awards and rave reviews. As development gets more and more difficult, the Pragmatic Programmers will be there with more titles and products to help you stay on top of your game.

Visit Us Online

This Book's Home Page
https://pragprog.com/book/aodjs
Source code from this book, errata, and other resources. Come give us feedback, too!

Keep Up-to-Date
https://pragprog.com
Join our announcement mailing list (low volume) or follow us on Twitter @pragprog for new titles, sales, coupons, hot tips, and more.

New and Noteworthy
https://pragprog.com/news
Check out the latest Pragmatic developments, new titles, and other offerings.

Save on the ebook

Save on the ebook versions of this title. Owning the paper version of this book entitles you to purchase the electronic versions at a terrific discount.

PDFs are great for carrying around on your laptop—they are hyperlinked, have color, and are fully searchable. Most titles are also available for the iPhone and iPod touch, Amazon Kindle, and other popular e-book readers.

Send a copy of your receipt to support@pragprog.com and we'll provide you with a discount coupon.

Contact Us

Online Orders:	*https://pragprog.com/catalog*
Customer Service:	*support@pragprog.com*
International Rights:	*translations@pragprog.com*
Academic Use:	*academic@pragprog.com*
Write for Us:	*http://write-for-us.pragprog.com*

www.ingramcontent.com/pod-product-compliance
Ingram Content Group UK Ltd.
Pitfield, Milton Keynes, MK11 3LW, UK
UKHW051855210426
470232UK00022B/186

9 798888 651988